AQA Media Studies

GCSE

Richard Morris
David Varley
Kevin Robinson
James McInerney

...hornes

Published in 2009 by:
Nelson Thornes Ltd
Delta Place
27 Bath Road
CHELTENHAM
GL53 7TH
United Kingdom

10 11 12 13 / 10 9 8 7 6 5 4 3 2

A catalogue record for this book is available from the British Library

ISBN 978 1 4085 0411 6

Cover photograph/illustration by Jupiter Images

Illustrations by AMR Design, Angela Knowles, Roger Penwill and Peters and Zabransky Ltd

Page make-up by AMR Design, (www.amrdesign.com)

Printed in China by 1010 Printing International Ltd.

Photo Acknowledgements

Eric Nathan/Alamy 7(b), Chris Ratcliffe/Rex 7(c), Rex Features 7(d), Alex Segre/ Alamy 7(e),15(c), Chris Batson/ Alamy 7(f), Sipa Press/Rex Features 7(g), Picture Partners/ Alamy 9 (a), 20th Century Fox/The Kobal Collection 8(marginal),11(c), Hill Street Studios/Blend Images/ Corbis 11(b), Tracy Kahn/Corbis 10(a), Edd Westmacott/Alamy 12(a), Margaret Bourke-White/Time & Life Pictures/Getty Images 14(a), Giles Moberly/ Alamy 15(b), Copyright BBC 15(d), David Crausby/Alamy 16(a-i), Joern Sackermann/ Alamy 16(a-ii), Glyn Thomas Photography/ Alamy 16(a-iii), Rick Maiman/Sygma/Corbis 17(centre), Carl Pendle/ Alamy 19(a), 20(a), Mike Kipling Photography / Alamy, Doable/amanaimages/ Corbis 20(margin), Phil Rees/Alamy 22(strip), Bauer Media 22(a), 23(c) 25(b), James Macari/Glamour© The Condé Nast Publications Ltd 23(b), Haymarket Media Group 24(a), Copyright Red magazine, published by Hachette Filipacchi UK Ltd 26(a), Wendy White/Alamy 30(a), D.C. Thompson & Co. Ltd. 32(a), 2000AD JudgeDredd ©& R Rebellion 33(b), Newmann/zefa/Corbis 40(margin), Fremantle Media 41(a), Copyright BBC 41(b, e), 51(b), Paramount Television/Isabella Vosmikova/The Kobal Collection 41 (c), Chris Clough, Company Productions Limited 41(d), Capital Pictures 41(f), NBCUPhotobank/Rex Features 43(a, b), Warner BrosTV/Bright/Kauffmann/Crane Pro / The Kobal Collection/Chris Haston 44(a), Gerardo Somoza/Corbis 45(b), Capital Pictures 46(a), CWNetworkEverett/Rex Features 47(b), Brian J. Ritchie/Rex Features 48(a), NBC-TV / The Kobal Collection / Paul Drinkwater 50(a), Action Press/Rex Features 59(a), Bedfordshire on Sunday 61(c), Clive Goddard/Cartoonstock 66(b), Andrew Patterson/Alamy 58(marginal), 67(c), Jeff McIntosh/Rex Features 67(d), Rex Features 67 (e), Ian McGregor/fotolia 76(strip), Ana Abejon/ Istockphoto 74 (marginal), MGM/United Artists/Sony/The Kobal Collection 76(a-i), T.Tulic/fotolia 76(a-ii), Devon Stephens/Istockphoto 76(a-iii), Steve Hammid/zefa/Corbis 76(a-iv), Spire FM 81(e), 20th Century Fox/Matt Groening/The Kobal Collection 91(b), Gaye Gerard/Getty Images 91(a), Keith Morris/Redferns 94(a), Bobby Bank/Redferns 94(b), Charlyn Zlotnik/Redferns 94(c), Deltahaze Corporation/Redferns 95(e-i), Tabatha Fireman/Redferns 95(e-ii), Bill Davila/Rex Features 90(marginal), 98(a), Gilles Petard Collection/Redferns 98(e-iii), Ebet Roberts/Redferns 98(e-v), GAB Archives / Redferns 98(ei-v), Joel Brodsky/Corbis 96(a), Richard Young/Rex Features 97(b), Ilpo Musto/Rex Features 97(c), Brian Rasic/Rex Features 100(a), Paul Bergen/Redferns 101(b), Eric Nathan / Alamy 106(marginal), The Advertising Archives 108(a), 109(b), 112(a), 113(b), Art Kowalsky / Alamy 117(a), Tree Line Films/Relativity Media /The Kobal Collection 124(a), Universal/The Kobal Collection 122(a), Focus Features /The Kobal Collection 123(c), Warner Bros/DC Comics/Kobal Collection 118-119(marginal and strip), 128(a,b), Rex Features 129(c), Movie Store Collection 120(a,b) 121(c) 122(b) 123 (d), New Line Cinema/Kobal Collection 127 (a,b) 131(a), Keith Morris/Alamy 135(a), Janine Wiedel Photolibrary/Alamy 136(b), Photodisc / Alamy 136(marginal), George Chamberlain/fotolia 138(marginal and strip), Frank Micelotta/Getty Images 143(a), Kevin Winter/Getty Images 143(b), Martin Asbury 145(a), Microsoft product box shot reprinted with permission from Microsoft Corporation 146, 147, JoeFox/ Alamy 149(b), Duncan ShawAlamy 149(b), Guitarist Magazine/Future Publishing 165(a), Waitrose Food Illustrated, November 2008 165(b), Mike Booth/Alamy 173(a), AQA copyright 175-185

Text Acknowledgements

Solo Syndication 6(a-i, ii) 63(c) 129(d), NRS 13(b), 63(e), Nuts/IPC Media 28(a), Chat/IPC Media 29(b), Telegraph Syndication 31(b), ABC 60(b), The Independent 62(a), News International 62(b) 129(e), Express Syndication 63(d) 64(a), 65(b), Eyetools Inc 79(c), :Hobbes' Internet Timeline and Netcraft Data 84(a), ABC/Eulogy 85(b), with permission of Kellogg Marketing and Sales Company (UK) Limited 110(a), www.adambanks.com 167(a), Bauer Media 75(a), courtesy Livelistingsmag.com 75(b), courtesy BBC Radio 1 78(a), Spire FM 78(b) 80(d), News International 157(b),

Student work

Kayleigh Hickman 35(a), 71(a), 73(a), 133(a), 139(a), 141(b), 162(marginal), 164(strip), 170(a), 171(a, b) Alison Morris 33(c), 36(a), 37(b), 54(a), Eli Palena 39(a), Wasim Akhtar 155(a), 158(a, b) 195(c)

The controlled assessment tasks in this book are designed to help you prepare for the tasks your teacher will give you. The tasks in this book are not designed to test you formally and you cannot use them as your own controlled assessment tasks for AQA. Your teacher will not be able to give you as much help with your tasks for AQA as we have given with the tasks in this book.

Contents

Nelson Thornes has worked in partnership with AQA to ensure this book and the accompanying online resources offer you the best support for your GCSE course.

All resources have been approved by senior AQA examiners so you can feel assured that they closely match the specification for this subject and provide you with everything you need to prepare successfully for your exams.

EXCLUSIVELY AQA ENDORSED

kerboodle!

These print and online resources together **unlock blended learning**; this means that the links between the activities in the book and the activities online blend together to maximise your understanding of a topic and help you achieve your potential.

These online resources are available on kerboodle! which can be accessed via the internet at **www.kerboodle.com/live**, anytime, anywhere. If your school or college subscribes to kerboodle! you will be provided with your own personal login details. Once logged in, access your course and locate the required activity.

For more information and help on how to use kerboodle! visit **www.kerboodle.com**.

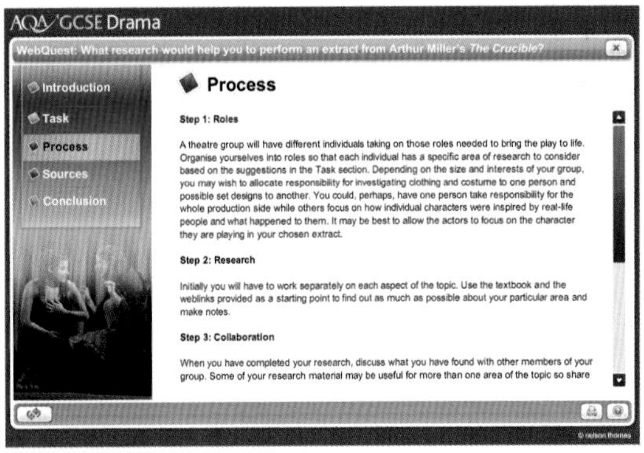

How to use this book

Objectives

Look for the list of **Learning Objectives** based on the requirements of this course so you can ensure you are covering everything you need to know for the exam.

AQA Examiner's tip

Don't forget to read the **AQA Examiner's Tips** throughout the book as well as practice answering **Examination-style Questions**.

Visit **www.nelsonthornes.com/aqagcse** for more information.

Why study the media?

With media studies getting so much publicity, it is important to ask the question, 'Why study the media?' Below is a list of eight possible answers. Do you agree with these reasons?

Students too dim for Media Studies
Daily Mail, 18 January 2007

Media Studies and other *Mickey Mouse degrees
Daily Mail, 12 September 2007

It's just watching films

A *Media Studies in the news*

*Mickey Mouse is a cultural icon of the 20th century. Created by Walt Disney in 1928, he became the best known and most widely recognised cartoon character in the United States. The Walt Disney Company today is a multi-million dollar, multi-national, media company. Clearly there is value in studying Mickey Mouse!

Reasons to study the media

Today the world is saturated by the mass media. To study the media is to understand the world we live in.

1 The mass media is very powerful. Advertisers and politicians use it to influence society. To be media literate is part of being an educated citizen.
2 Education has traditionally concentrated on literacy. In today's society, the visual image is as important as the printed word. Students of media studies learn to read and construct visual images.
3 The ability to design, construct and edit media products are relevant, modern, practical skills. Skilled media studies students are employable.
4 The media is an expanding industry. GCSE media studies can help start students on the road to careers in the media.
5 GCSE media studies develops critical thinking, analytical skills and creativity.
6 GCSE media studies develops group work skills.
7 We spend a large proportion of our time exposed to the media. GCSE media studies helps us examine the impact the media has on our lives.
8 Because the media studies us!

Did you know ??????

It is estimated that 97 per cent of the UK population own a television. 75 per cent of the UK population read a daily newspaper.

Discussion activity

1 Read the eight reasons to study the media and discuss with the rest of your class:
- a How important is it to study the media?
- b How does the media study us?

We live in a world saturated by the mass media

B *Advertising*

C *Politics*

D *Television celebrities*

E *Web-based media*

F *Newspapers*

G *The film industry*

1 GCSE Media Studies at a glance

GCSE Media Studies

Unit 1 Investigating the media (External assessment)

This is a 1 hour 30 minute examination in June, worth 60 marks; 40 per cent of the GCSE marks.

Each year a different media topic will be set for students to research. In the exam you will be required to demonstrate your knowledge of the set topic through written responses to questions and creative responses such as **storyboarding** or writing a **script**, working to a set brief.

Unit 2 Understanding the media (Controlled assessment)

This consists of three coursework tasks taken from banks of set assignments, worth 90 marks; 60 per cent of the GCSE marks.

Assignment 1 Introduction to the media

Your teacher will choose one assignment from a bank of eight. You will then be expected to:

- Analyse one or two media texts using approximately 400 words.
- Carry out a research and planning task that will involve you presenting ideas for a text in the same **genre** as the media text(s) you have analysed.
- Demonstrate an understanding of audience.
- Briefly explain your ideas and how they would appeal to your audience using approximately 100 words.
- Use media terminology and show awareness of media language.

Assignment 1 is marked out of 15.

Assignment 2 Cross-media study

Your teacher will choose one assignment from a bank of six. You will then be expected to:

- Analyse, using approximately 800 words, two texts as part of a media campaign.
- Consider media texts as part of a **cross-media campaign**.
- Respond to two texts that are connected or part of the same campaign: one will be a print- or web-based text (so you will be dealing with mostly 'still' images such as those in magazines, newspapers or on websites); the other will be an audio-visual text (such as a video or radio text).

Key terms

Storyboarding: often used as a planning tool by professional film makers. It involves drawing a sequence of illustrations that represents the shots planned for a film or television production.

Script: the written text of a play, film or broadcast.

Genre: from the French meaning 'type'. When we talk about a genre of film, we might refer to science fiction, romantic comedy or several other 'types' of film.

Cross-media campaign: when the same text appears on a range of different platforms. For instance, the release of a new film will result in a media-wide campaign with material generated across different forms, such as television, radio, magazines, newspapers and the internet.

Key concepts: in GCSE Media Studies these are media language, audience, representation and institutions. See pages 10–17.

- Research, plan and design your own cross-media campaign in the same topic area. This will involve presenting ideas for a print- or web-based text and an audio-visual piece, which will complement each other.
- Demonstrate your understanding of media language and audience as well as your understanding of representation and institutional factors.
- Explain your ideas using approximately 200 words.

Assignment 2 is marked out of 30.

Assignment 3 Practical production

Your teacher will choose one assignment from a bank of six. You will then be expected to:

- Produce your own media text.
- Present evidence of research and planning (up to 12 pages).
- You have the option to work in a small group, depending on which assignment is chosen.
- Use original material wherever possible. For instance, original photographs for magazines, newspapers and websites.
- Keep your productions to strict time or page limits. For instance, a film trailer should be no more than two minutes long.
- Write a 700–800 word evaluation to reflect on the strengths and weaknesses of the production.
- Demonstrate awareness of all **key concepts**.

Assignment 3 is marked out of 45.

A *You might create your own website as part of AQA GCSE Media Studies*

links

For information on the four key concepts, see pages 10–17.

kerboodle!

1.1 Media language

AQA GCSE Media Studies is centred around four key concepts: media language, audience, representation and institutions. This topic focuses on media language.

Objectives

To gain an understanding of media language and to be able to apply this knowledge to media texts you will study.

Reading the signs – denotation and connotation

In analysing media texts, we need to think about the messages offered by something that we see (or hear, in the case of audio texts). If the thing we see is the sign, then the ideas, impressions or messages it gives us are what is signified. An example would be if it were raining. The rain is the sign, but rain tends to have fairly sad or miserable associations. So what is signified by the rain might be sadness. You can quickly work out what might be signified if the sign is the sun. Obviously there are lots of different possible interpretations to each sign. Rain can be linked to romance, while the sun might signify burning or drought.

When looking at a media text we are expected to try and read these signs because they add meaning. One method that is popular with students is to think in terms of **denotation** and **connotation**. Denotation is what is there. Connotation is what it might mean or suggest. Look at the examples below. These are oversimplified but you should get the idea!

A *Denotation: a young man wearing sunglasses*

Connotations of sunglasses:

- Looking cool, laid-back and relaxed
- Suggestion of being wealthy, fashionable, confident and attractive
- Might also suggest summer/holidays.

These are all fairly positive connotations.

B *Denotation: a young man wearing spectacles*

Connotations of spectacles:

- Geeky, intelligent, less confident physically
- Formal
- Stiff
- Less attractive.

These are mostly negative connotations.

Applying the terminology

Each media form has its own technical terms or media language, e.g. newspapers have headlines and by-lines. It's impossible to cover all examples, but the terminology relating to different media forms, such as the internet, will be explained within the relevant chapters of this book. However, most media texts feature images: you need to know some of the key terms relating to the different types of shot used in film, television, magazines or newspapers.

Shot types include:

- Long shot
- Medium shot
- Close-up
- High angle
- Low angle
- Point of view.

These shots can have their own connotations. A close-up is more intimate and personal. A low-angled shot makes objects look bigger and more powerful. You will gain marks for using technical terms in your analysis, but you need to read the signs and interpret the meanings in order to achieve the higher grades.

C *What type of shot is this?*

Activity

Apply denotation and connotation to the film poster in **C**.

1.2 Audience

Identifying the audience

This topic focuses on another of the four key concepts: **audience**.

In a cinema or at a concert it's easy to say who the audience is – the people looking at the screen or the stage! But who are they really? They have one thing in common – they all turned up to be entertained at the same time. But do they have any other similarities? For instance, if you go to see a horror movie at the cinema on a Friday evening you'll probably find that most of the audience will be aged 16–25. That doesn't mean that there aren't any people over the age of 25, or that they shouldn't go to the cinema. It just means that different films, like magazines and newspapers, attract different audiences.

In your class you'll have people or groups of people who have different tastes. You may be the same age but sometimes that's where the similarity ends. Whatever 'group' you belong to you'll probably consume different media texts from your friends. You'll listen to different music, watch different films, and so on. It's probably the same at home. Just because you share the same house, it's unlikely that you'll watch the same television programmes as members of your family.

Objectives

To gain an understanding of audience and to be able to apply this knowledge to media texts you will study.

How media producers research their audience

A media product can't exist without an audience – well, not for very long. Media producers need to know that there is an audience out there and they spend a great deal of time and money finding out who their audience is.

They categorise people into different groups according to age, ethnicity, gender, where they live, their occupation and income, their education and lifestyle choices, their attitudes and political persuasions. There are lots of other categories too.

One way of categorising audience is by occupation and income according to the social grade classification used by the National Readership Survey. The classification groups people according to their social status and the amount of money they earn. It identifies six groups, as shown in table **B**.

A *What does this audience have in common?*

B *National Readership Survey's social grade classification*

Social grade	Social status	Chief income earner's profession
A	Upper middle class	Higher managerial, administrative or professional. Doctors and lawyers
B	Middle class	Intermediate managerial, administrative or professional. Managers and teachers
C1	Lower middle class	Non-manual workers. Office workers
C2	Skilled working class	Skilled manual workers. Plumbers and electricians
D	Working class	Semi-skilled and unskilled manual workers. Shop assistants, farm and building site labourers
E	Unemployed/receiving benefits	Casual workers (not in regular employment). Pensioners and others who depend on the state for their income

This scale is problematic in a number of ways but it is still widely used (look at the reader profiles from magazines on pages 28–29). Many people feel insulted by being categorised in this way. The scale is limited in that it assumes each household or family has a single main earner (probably male) and that all in the family have similar tastes. It also classifies students as being part of group E, when most are from a much higher background and are probably headed for jobs much higher up the scale. However, with 60 million people in Britain it was never going to be easy fitting them all into six categories!

How audiences use media texts

Another important aspect of audience study is to consider how audiences use media texts. Some television programmes are watched closely and thoughtfully and make us think about issues of importance. Other programmes offer a chance to relax and forget about our troubles. In the 1970s, media theorists Blumler and Katz presented their model of audience **uses and gratifications**, declaring that there were five main reasons why audiences consumed media texts:

1. To be informed and educated
2. In order to identify with characters and situations
3. To be entertained
4. To enable themselves to socially interact with others (by watching, listening or reading together or through discussion of what they'd seen, read or heard)
5. To escape from their daily troubles and woes.

Activity

Think of one TV programme and one print publication that you do not watch or read – who is the audience?

1.3 Representation

What is representation?

Representation is the third key concept. **Representation** in the media is concerned with how people, events and ideas are presented to audiences. What we see, hear and read in the media is a representation of a subject. Even a live broadcast is a representation, because you only see what is filmed by the camera operator. As a media studies student, it is important that you are able to identify and understand these representations.

Objectives

To gain an understanding of representation and to able to apply this knowledge to media texts you will study.

Why is representation important?

The media often claim that they show reality. Gritty soap operas are meant to be true to life, 'reality TV' claims to follow the lives of 'real' people, and magazines expose the 'real' lives of celebrities. However none of this is truly real; they are all versions of reality edited and packaged by the media. It is the media that decide how to represent people and events and, as a result, they have an enormous potential influence and impact on their audience.

Representations can have a positive and negative effect. People can be portrayed as heroes or villains. The way they look can be airbrushed and altered, and what they say can be edited. Sometimes representations can reinforce stereotypes and erode the self image of people. So, when studying the media, you need to think critically about how people and events are represented, misrepresented and unrepresented.

Questions of representation

When analysing a media text, here are some questions to consider when looking at representation:

- How have different genders been represented?
- How have different age groups been represented?
- How have different races or religions been represented?
- Have any groups been unrepresented? If so, why?
- How accurate is the representation?
- Can the representation be interpreted in different ways?
- Who has constructed the representation and why?
- What effect does the representation have on the intended audience?

A *The billboard presents a representation of life in America in the 1930s*

A representation of young people in the media

How do you feel when you see young people portrayed in the media? Do you feel young people are fairly represented, or does the media present inaccurate stereotypes?

Activities

B

C

D

1 How accurately do these images represent young people in Britain?

2 Do these images give a positive or negative image of young people?

3 Do you think young people are fairly represented in the media?

Extension activities

1 Using current newspapers, cut out any stories that are about young people in Britain.

2 Examine how young people are represented in each article and divide the news stories into three piles: positive, neutral and negative.

3 What do your findings tell you about the representation of young people in newspapers?

1.4 Institutions

What are media institutions?

Media institutions are organisations that are responsible for producing media products. Think of your favourite film, album, video game or television programme: each one was produced by a media company. Have you ever noticed the names of these businesses? Some of them are huge multi-national companies, while others might be small-scale, independent companies.

Why are media institutions important?

An important aspect of understanding a media text is to understand who has produced it and why. Every media institution will have its own set of values, and these are often evident in the media products they produce. For example, ITV is Britain's largest terrestrial commercial television network. ITV relies on advertising to pay for its programmes. To maintain funding from advertisers, ITV has to produce programmes that will appeal to mass audiences in the UK. Therefore, you will notice that ITV produces a number of popular mass-appeal programmes such as *The X Factor, Who Wants to be a Millionaire?, Coronation Street* and *Emmerdale.*

Objectives

To gain an understanding of media institutions and to be able to apply this knowledge to media texts you will study.

Group activities

1 Select one area of the media from the list below:

Film	Music
Television	Radio
Magazines	Video games

2 List as many media institutions as you can that are associated with your chosen area.

3 Can you think of any media institutions that are involved in several areas of the media?

A Some logos of well-known media institutions

News Corporation

News Corporation is one of the world's largest media institutions. In fact it is made up of a number of media companies. The institution's chairman is Rupert Murdoch. Revenue for the year ending June 2007 was $28.6 billion.

Here are just some of the media companies owned by News Corporation.

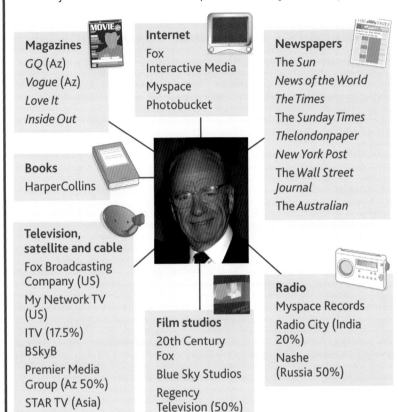

Magazines
GQ (Az)
Vogue (Az)
Love It
Inside Out

Internet
Fox Interactive Media
Myspace
Photobucket

Newspapers
The *Sun*
News of the World
The Times
The *Sunday Times*
Thelondonpaper
New York Post
The *Wall Street Journal*
The *Australian*

Books
HarperCollins

Television, satellite and cable
Fox Broadcasting Company (US)
My Network TV (US)
ITV (17.5%)
BSkyB
Premier Media Group (Az 50%)
STAR TV (Asia)

Film studios
20th Century Fox
Blue Sky Studios
Regency Television (50%)

Radio
Myspace Records
Radio City (India 20%)
Nashe (Russia 50%)

Did you know ??????

In 1998, Rupert Murdoch tried to buy Manchester United for £625 million. But the offer was rejected by the UK Competition Commission.

Activities

1. Look at the illustration showing the companies owned by News Corporation.
2. Identify how News Corporation is a multi-national institution.
3. Rupert Murdoch used to be a strong supporter of the Conservative Party. How do you think he might have used his media empire to help the Conservative Party?
4. Why do you think some people argue that it is dangerous for one institution to control so many areas of the media?

Regulation and control

While some media institutions are very powerful, governments have put some limits on what these organisations can say and do. Laws, such as libel, protect people from being falsely accused. It is common to see media institutions being sued by people in the public eye. In most areas of the media, there are regulatory bodies set up to control the output of media institutions. For instance, the British Board of Film Classification (BBFC) controls the certification of films in Britain. The Office of Communication (Ofcom) regulates television and radio. In 2007 Ofcom received over 44 000 complaints regarding racial issues in *Celebrity Big Brother*.

The media also self-regulate. An example of self-regulation is the Press Complaints Commission, which is responsible for dealing with complaints that members of the public make about a newspaper. To fully understand media institutions, it is important to understand the regulations and limitations under which they operate.

Extension activities

Research a media institution of your choice:

1. How and when did it begin?
2. What products does it produce?
3. Does the institution own other media institutions?
4. How profitable is the institution?
5. Who runs the institution?
6. How is the institution regulated and controlled?

GCSE

The controlled assessment

Assignment 1. Introduction to the media

This assignment is titled 'Introduction to the media' and the intention is that you begin to develop a critical approach to media texts. This means that instead of simply watching, reading or listening for enjoyment you adopt a more serious and studious approach. This will involve you looking at a media text very closely in order to identify the key features, consider audience appeal and think about the messages that might be given. It might help if you actually enjoy the text you're looking at or listening to, but you won't earn any marks for simply saying that something is 'brilliant' or that something else is 'boring'.

Eight topics can be studied for Assignment 1 and this unit will focus on four of them: print (magazines and newspapers), children's comics, moving image (television programmes) and web-based media. In these topics you will analyse the **codes and conventions** of different media texts and be introduced to many key terms. The key concepts of media language and audience are to be addressed in this assignment. References to representation and institutions might be considered something of a bonus.

Objectives

To learn about the first controlled assessment assignment for Unit 2 of AQA GCSE Media Studies.

Key terms

Codes and conventions: the typical features that we would expect from a particular text, the 'rules'.

Narrative: the story – a sequence of events.

Secondary audience: not the main, expected audience for a media text but another group who might be part of the audience. For instance, teenage girls' magazines sometimes interest the brothers or boyfriends of the main target audience. They are a secondary audience.

A *Recording*

What do you need to do?

You will study one media topic and:

- Focus on the key concepts of media language and audience.
- Apply media terminology.
- Identify how genre is established.
- Discuss how **narrative** is suggested.
- Make judgements about who the target audience might be.
- Identify a possible **secondary audience** or consider how the product might be consumed.

All of the above should then enable you to complete the required analysis, which should be approximately 400 words.

You will then need to:

- Work in the same topic area to present a pre-production task based on the same genre of media and aimed at a specific audience.
- Explain how the product would appeal to its target audience using approximately 100 words.

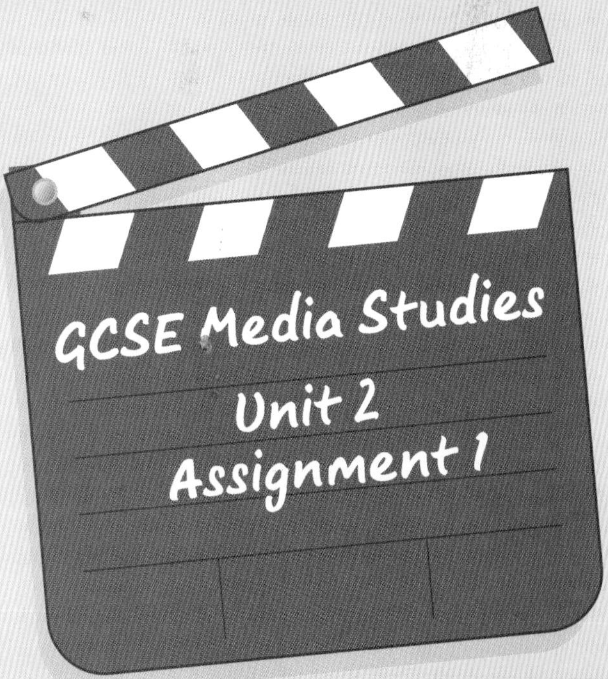

B *Preparing for action*

kerboodle!

2 Magazines

Objectives

To learn about what is required for the analysis of magazine front covers.

About this topic

What you will need to do

If you or your teacher chooses magazines or comics for Assignment 1, you will be required to write about two different magazine front covers or two different comic front covers. To do this successfully you'll need to analyse the front covers closely, using media terminology and considering the way the magazine or comic catches the attention of its audience. There's no need to compare the covers to anything else or to write about historical developments (how magazines or comics have changed over time). You'll need to focus purely on the front covers you or your teacher choose.

You have only 400 words in which to write your responses. It would be very easy to write an explanation of what you can see but, in order to achieve high marks, you can't just write anything that comes into your head!

A breakdown of the tasks

Here's a useful breakdown of what you will be required to do:

- Write about the typical codes and conventions of the genre of the front covers.
- Show understanding of aspects of media language.
- Use technical terms.
- Say something about representation.
- Consider the effect the covers have on the audience.

Following this you'll be asked to present ideas for a magazine or comic of your own in the same genre. Using what you've learned about magazines or comics you will write a brief report (no more than 100 words) on your ideas.

Masses of magazines

If you take time to look in your local newsagent or supermarket you will be amazed at just how many magazines are on sale. It's hard to believe that all of them can find enough readers to stay in business! That doesn't take account of all the magazines that are given away free – by far the majority. Every shop, business or trade seems to have its own magazine.

AQA GCSE media studies requires you to look at mass media texts, so we will be looking at the sort of publications you find in the newsagents rather than trade magazines such as *Hotel and Caterer*. These are called consumer magazines and they tend to fall into a number of categories or genres. In one supermarket the categories of consumer magazine were:

- TV listings – originally just the *Radio Times* and the *TV Times* but now a number of magazines carry guides to what's on TV
- Special interest
- Women's interest
- Men's lifestyle
- Weeklies
- Children's
- Entertainment
- Homes and gardens
- Computing
- Motoring.

Starter activity

Find out the name of at least one magazine for each category of consumer magazine listed above.

Magazine publishers have their own categories, too. For instance, the smaller, handbag-sized magazines such as *Glamour* are referred to as 'baby glossies'!

A *What draws you to the magazines that you read?*

AQA Examiner's tip

You shouldn't just rely on your first impressions or on whether you like the front cover or not. It is important to have your own view, but describing something simply as 'boring' or 'safe' isn't really appropriate for a GCSE response.

kerboodle!

2.1 Understanding magazine covers

What's on magazine front covers?

The main purpose of the front cover of a magazine, as with newspapers, books and other media, is to sell the magazine by making it look appealing. Even so, magazine front covers tend to follow a very similar pattern or formula. The typical ingredients rarely change. Here we are going to look at four main components of magazine front covers: masthead, sell lines, main image and covermount.

Objectives

To learn about the codes and conventions and the technical terms associated with magazine front covers.

Masthead

The name of the magazine will be at the top of the front cover page and will be clearly seen. This is the **masthead**. It acts as a kind of logo or symbol for the magazine and will mostly stay the same. The colour might be changed to suit the colour scheme of the rest of the cover or the time of year, but the **font**, size of lettering and the positioning will be fixed.

Key terms

Font: the style of lettering used.

Sell lines

Sometimes called 'cover lines', the sell lines are the writing that appears around the main image and which tell readers what is inside the magazine. Sometimes the sell lines can be shocking or exciting or humerous. Emotive words are used to attract readers' attention. However, you could argue that the sell lines are there to reassure and offer few surprises.

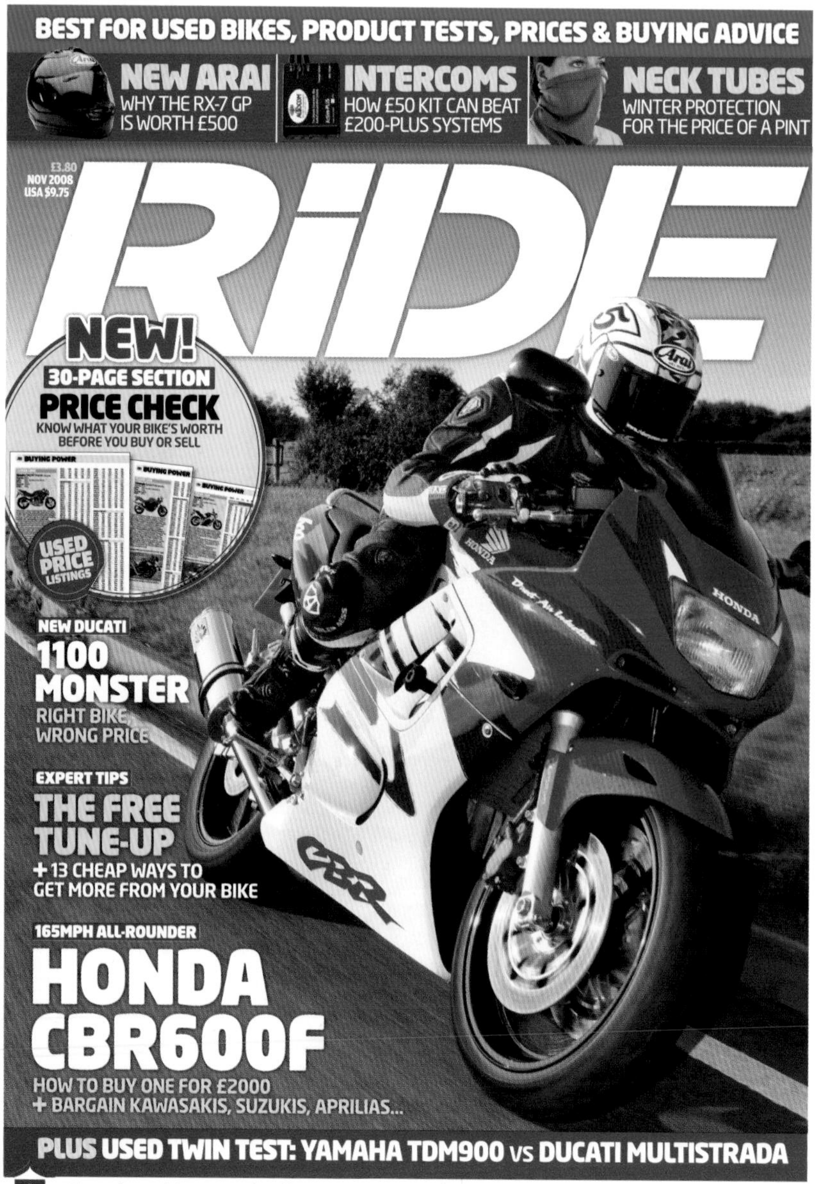

A *How does this magazine front cover appeal to motorbiking enthusiasts?*

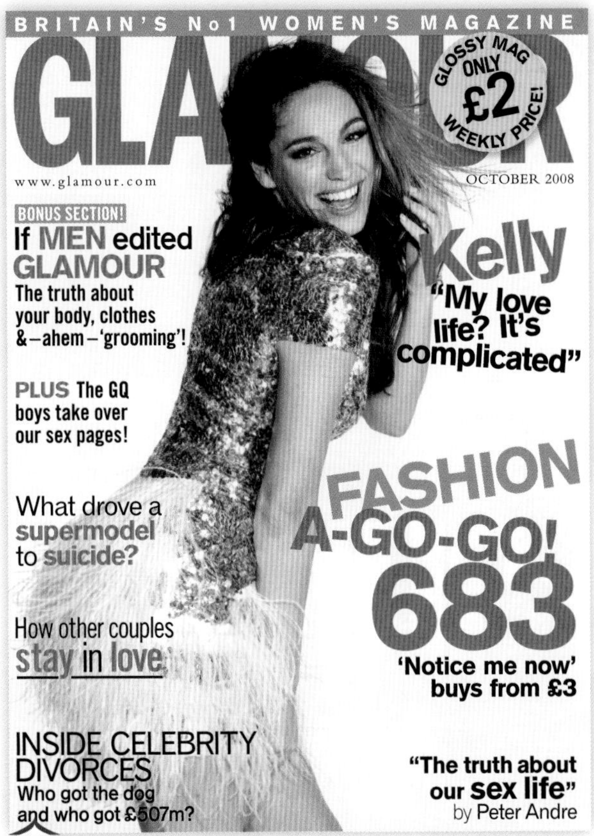

B *A front cover of* Glamour *magazine*

C *The 'busy' front cover of* Heat *magazine*

Main image

Most magazines feature a single portrait photograph as the central focus of the front cover. The sell lines and other features are usually arranged around it. Both *Ride* and *Glamour* (see front covers **A** and **B**) use this type of layout. Magazines like *Heat* (see front cover **C**) and *Closer* use a number of different images and the covers appear more busy and cluttered.

Covermount

This is a 'free gift' mounted on the cover of a magazine to increase sales. Sometimes the 'gift' is wrapped in an outer sleeve.

The 'gift' will depend on the magazine. The women's magazine *Red* might give away a 'chick lit' novel, whereas the football magazine *Match!* might offer free stickers of footballers. More expensive music magazines like *Q* and *Mojo* often come with a free CD. What covermounted 'free gifts' have you received with a magazine?

Activities

1. Look at the masthead of *Ride* magazine. How does the masthead suit the magazine?
2. Pick out three sell lines from this front cover of *Glamour* that would appeal to the magazine's readers. Do the sell lines offer any shocks or surprises, or are they what you would expect to see on the front cover of this magazine?
3. Which front cover works best: the single picture portrait layout of *Glamour* magazine or the busier layout of *Heat*? What are the advantages and disadvantages of each type of front cover?

kerboodle!

2.2 The features of magazine covers

Objectives

To look at how codes and conventions are used on the front cover of a particular magazine and to consider the layout of the page.

Masthead

In your analysis, you might comment on the size, colour and font of the masthead. It's also important to say something about the choice of title.

Skyline

Runs across the top of the page and calls out to readers about some special attraction(s).

Slogan

Often a boast claiming that the magazine is special or unique.

Anchorage text

The main image features lots of famous players and the text tells us why they are featured here on the cover. All this is a lure to read the article inside the magazine about them.

A *How does the layout of this front cover appeal to football supporters?*

Strapline

A strap or bar of information that runs across the top of the page.

Price

Notice how small the price is printed! When magazines are cheap, the price will be really large so that you notice it. But here …

Main image

Why have these players been chosen and why is Ronaldo in the middle? Why does the main image overlap the name of the magazine? What type of shot makes up the main image: a long shot or medium shot?

Sell lines

A range of football topics are mentioned from around the world and there are references to players and managers from the past. This might suggest that the magazine is aimed at fans who are serious about the game, who might be older, and who might want to read detailed articles.

Bar code

Magazines have a bar code on the front cover; books have a bar code on the back.

Layout

This cover is quite formal in its organisation. It's all straight lines and fairly orderly. That could suggest that it's aimed at older, more thoughtful and serious football supporters. Other magazines 'shout' more to their readers and use more effects, including:

- graphic effects such as shapes and arrows
- text and boxes at different angles
- puffs in the corners of pages which exclaim about other content
- direct address to the audience, e.g. 'you', 'your' or 'you will'.

If you compare the front cover of *FourFourTwo* with the front cover of *Match!* (see front cover **B**), aimed at a much younger reader, you'll see a big difference.

Colour scheme

The colours of the photographs dominate but font colours have been chosen to complement these. Despite the rather bright yellows, the colours here are ones that seem quite male oriented. The red, black and white tend to have football connotations.

Direct address?

Most magazine covers feature a person making direct eye contact with the readers to achieve intimacy. This isn't always the case with sports magazines, where action shots are used rather than posed photographs.

B Match! *football magazine*

Activity

Identify four reasons why Match! would appeal to a younger audience than *FourFourTwo*.

2.3 Analysing magazine front covers

Going into detail

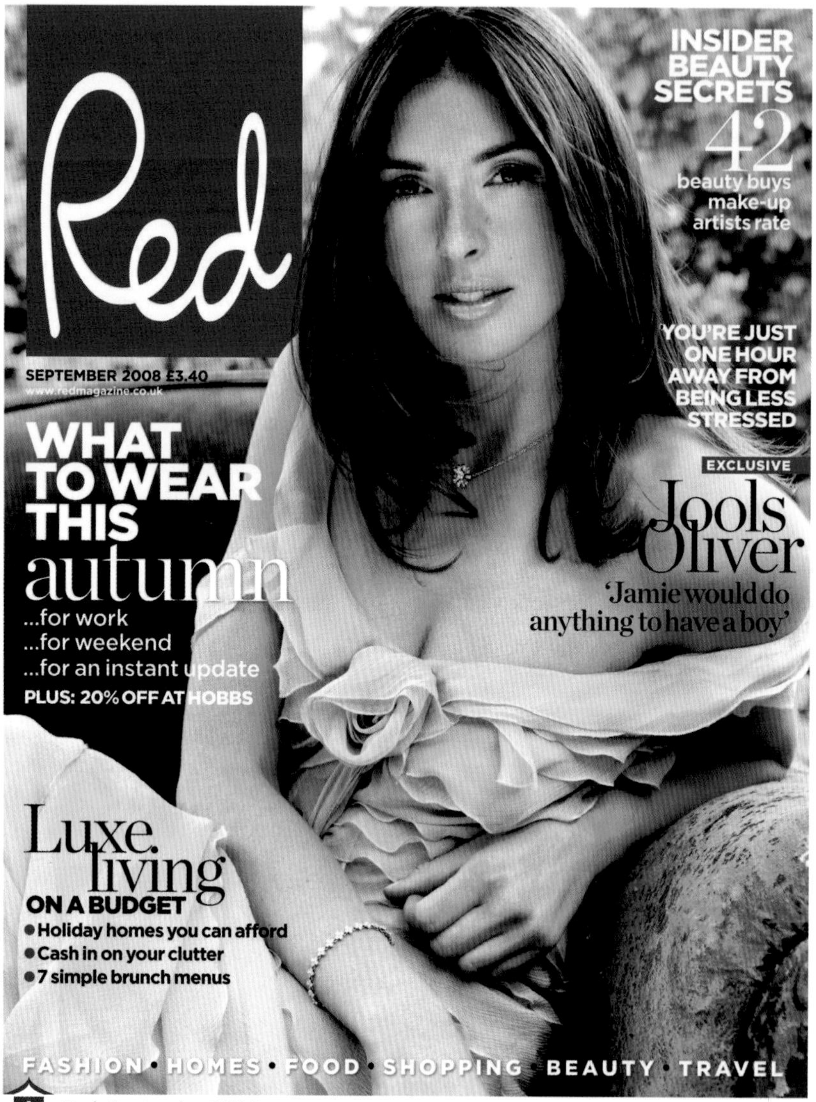

A Red, *September 2008*

When writing about magazine front covers you need to answer lots of questions. These are likely to begin with 'What?' or 'Why?'.

Here is a simple example of this using the front cover of *Red* from September 2008.

Objectives

To apply the technical terms to the analysis of magazine front covers.

Question

What can I see on the cover?

There is a photograph of Juliette 'Jools' Oliver, wife of TV chef Jamie. It is a medium-long shot. She is looking at the camera, giving direct address. She has a faint smile and is wearing what looks like an expensive necklace and bracelet. She is wearing a cream dress and the sleeves are falling down, particularly on her left shoulder, so the dress is quite revealing.

The masthead for the magazine says the name Red in white letters on a red background. The font is serif which means that it is quite fancy writing but it appears to have been hand-written. These letters and the colours will be the same every month.

There are 112 words here that focus on the main image and on the masthead. Clearly there is plenty more that the student could have written about but we aren't looking at that here. In this extract, the detail and use of technical terminology might be enough to earn this response a low C grade. The response is mainly descriptive; it tells us *what* is there but makes no attempt to say *why* it is there. For a real analytical response you need to think of some 'why?' questions.

Here are two:

- Why has Jools Oliver been chosen for the front cover?
- Why has the publisher used red and white for the masthead and for some of the sell lines?

Once you have thought of some 'Why?' questions you may have a problem – you don't know all of the answers! Still, it's likely that you'll have some of them. There can be lots of answers; three answers to the first question appear below. You might have only got one of these answers, but do the others make sense too?

Question

Why has Jools Oliver been chosen for the front cover?

1 Because she has become something of a celebrity herself through her marriage to Jamie Oliver. People recognise her.

2 As a wife and mother, she is someone that the magazine's target audience can relate to.

3 Readers would see her as slim, attractive, wealthy and successful. All of which they might aspire to be themselves.

If you have questions that you can't answer, you probably need to think in terms of how the magazine is trying to appeal to its readers. Questions like: 'Why is she sitting on a battered looking sofa?' or 'Why has the photograph been taken outdoors?' can only be answered by considering who the magazine is aimed at. That's our next task. To consider who the readers might be.

Activities

1 With a partner, try to think of five more 'why' questions for the *Red* front cover.

2 The other 'Why?' question asked of the *Red* front cover was: 'Why has the publisher used red and white for the masthead and for some of the sell lines?' Try to answer this question. Offer more than one response if you can. Think about the connotations these colours might carry.

Key terms

Serif: a slight projection finishing off the stroke of a letter. Letters presented in a serif font are curly and appear traditional or old fashioned.

2.4 Magazine audience profiling

Magazines don't have just one audience, however, a **core audience** can usually be identified. At a very simple level, we can often tell whether a magazine is for men or women. It's usually easy to guess the age of the core audience – whether pre-school, teen or adult. But why does it matter? Anyone can buy any magazine if they choose to.

It is mainly magazine publishers who need to identify the **demographic** for a particular publication, in order to maximise the effectiveness and value of their advertising. Magazines cannot survive on the revenue from the cover price and need to attract advertisers to their magazine. They can do this more effectively if they know who will be reading the magazine. For instance, a teenage girls' magazine such as *More* or *Sugar* will include adverts for products that teenage girls are likely to buy: hair and make-up products, mobile phones and chocolate. The magazine publishers can charge the advertisers more for the advertising, because they can guarantee that the adverts will reach the appropriate audience.

A *All about* Nuts *readers*

Objectives

To learn about how a magazine targets, and is used by, its audience.

Did you know ??????

It costs £10 200 to take out a one-page advertisement in *Nuts* magazine. A double-page spread advertisement in *Chat* magazine costs £21 500!

Key terms

Core audience: the main audience of a media text.

Demographic: measurement of the population in terms of age, sex, religion, income, ethnicity, etc.

ABCe Unique Users figure: tells you how many different people visit a magazine's website in a month.

Index: the National Readership Survey interviews approximately 30 000 people a year about their reading habits. From this an index is compiled. Figures over 100 show that readers are 'more likely' than non-readers to fit a certain profile.

There are many interesting things we can learn from the *Nuts* audience profile:

- 85 per cent of *Nuts* readers are male.
- Using the National Readership Survey's Social Grade classification (pages 12–13) 74 per cent of them are categorised as B, C1 or C2.
- According to the **ABCe Unique Users figure**, almost as many people visit the *Nuts* website as read the magazine.

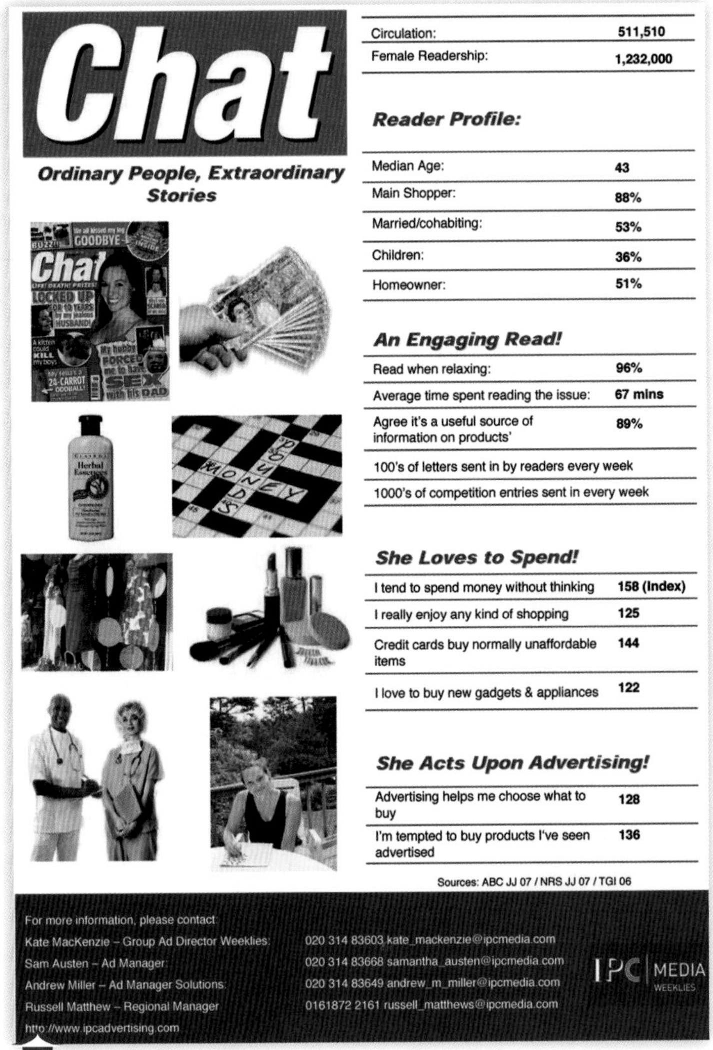

Chat

Ordinary People, Extraordinary Stories

Circulation:	511,510
Female Readership:	1,232,000

Reader Profile:

Median Age:	43
Main Shopper:	88%
Married/cohabiting:	53%
Children:	36%
Homeowner:	51%

An Engaging Read!

Read when relaxing:	96%
Average time spent reading the issue:	67 mins
Agree it's a useful source of information on products'	89%
100's of letters sent in by readers every week	
1000's of competition entries sent in every week	

She Loves to Spend!

I tend to spend money without thinking	158 (Index)
I really enjoy any kind of shopping	125
Credit cards buy normally unaffordable items	144
I love to buy new gadgets & appliances	122

She Acts Upon Advertising!

Advertising helps me choose what to buy	128
I'm tempted to buy products I've seen advertised	136

Sources: ABC JJ 07 / NRS JJ 07 / TGI 06

For more information, please contact:

Kate MacKenzie – Group Ad Director Weeklies: 020 314 83603 kate_mackenzie@ipcmedia.com

Sam Austen – Ad Manager: 020 314 83668 samantha_austen@ipcmedia.com

Andrew Miller – Ad Manager Solutions: 020 314 83649 andrew_m_miller@ipcmedia.com

Russell Matthew – Regional Manager 0161872 2161 russell_matthews@ipcmedia.com

http://www.ipcadvertising.com

IPC MEDIA WEEKLIES

B *All about* Chat *readers*

What statistics relating to *Chat* magazine are the most remarkable? Is it that over a million women read *Chat?* Or that the average age of the readers is 47? Or that, according to the **index** figure, *Chat* readers love to shop!

Uses and gratifications

The section, 'An engaging read', in the audience profile for *Chat* magazine gives some sense of how and why readers might use *Chat*: to relax, to get information and (by sending in and reading letters) to feel part of a community. How does this fit in with Blumler and Katz's uses and gratifications theory?

Activity

Magazines construct audience profiles in order to encourage companies to buy advertising space in their publication. Look at the reader profiles for *Nuts* and *Chat* and make a list of 10 products that you would expect to see advertised in these magazines.

Research activity

Use the internet to search for other reader profiles. You'll need to know who has published the magazine, which you can usually find out by looking at the contents page or inside back cover: **www.ipcmedia.com/magazines** is a good place to start.

links

Refer back to pages 12–13 on audience, and in particular to the reference to Blumler and Katz's theory of uses and gratifications.

2.5 Representation in magazines

Looking back at the previous topic on audience profiles it's clear that magazines have an idea of what particular groups of society are like. *Nuts* readers are young-ish males who are interested in girls, football and fashion. *Chat* readers are women and they are mainly interested in shopping! This can give rise to stereotypical depictions, where we see a group of people as having a narrow range of fairly obvious characteristics. Magazines have often been criticised for presenting a limited or narrow view and for encouraging readers to conform to lifestyle expectations.

Objectives

To learn about how magazines represent people.

The camera never lies?

The front cover of the January 2003 issue of *GQ*, a men's lifestyle magazine, caused a great deal of controversy because it featured a retouched image of *Titanic* star Kate Winslet, making her appear much slimmer than in real life. Critics claimed that this representation would encourage young girls to think that they had to be thin to be successful and would increase eating disorders among young girls. Even without the retouching, you could argue that the cover presented a very stereotypical image of women.

A *Spot the difference: before retouching and after*

Activity

Look at the front covers of 10 women's magazines. Like men's magazines, these almost always feature women. What do they look like? What groups of people are represented or not represented? What messages about women do these images offer?

Extension activity

Compare the representation of women on the covers of men's magazines and women's magazines. What are the differences and similarities?

Telling you who to be?

Media representations are very influential and many believe that this influence can be damaging. Teenage girls' magazines are often criticised because they seem to suggest that life revolves around how you look and finding a boyfriend. Whichever magazines you study, you'll need to consider some aspects of representation. For instance, celebrities are often represented as heroes and role models in magazines such as *Heat* and *Now*.

Are lads' mags bad?

So-called 'lads' mags' like *Nuts* and *Zoo* have been criticised for their representation of women. The readers are of a relatively young age and it is argued that some young males will be encouraged to treat women in a sexist manner as a result of reading these magazines. A stereotypical view of women as being young, slim, well endowed and sexually available is presented. There's no depth or variety to this portrayal and it seems that the only woman who are valued are the glamour models that are featured. 'Valued' may not be the best term! Look at the article below from *The Telegraph* in 2008, which followed a Member of Parliament's complaints about 'lads' mags'.

links

Refer back to pages 14–15 on representation.

Mags that demean lads and lasses

By Liz Hunt

Lads' mags are under attack again. Shadow schools secretary Michael Gove blames them for portraying women as "permanently, lasciviously, uncomplicatedly available". No wonder so many young men view women as sex objects, he says. No wonder we have a generation of feckless fathers who hot foot it at the merest hint of a family value.

He is right, of course. Such magazines assault the eye and insult women on a daily basis. They coarsen our culture, devalue relationships and promote a sexual free-for-all.

Gove implied that men were largely to blame for this state of affairs, and that the Gemmas, Michelles and Biancas who (dis) grace the pages of Nuts, Zoo, Loaded and the like are being exploited. He praised women's magazines for the "mature and responsible" manner in which they addressed their readers. That is where he lost me. How long ago was it that Mr Gove last ventured into a newsagent's? Has he not seen row upon row of glossy "slag mags" that glorify the antics of those members of the sisterhood who seem to have no problem with appearing to be "permanently, lasciviously, uncomplicatedly available". Women are just as culpable as men in this tawdry business – if not more so, because they should know better.

B

2.6 Comics

Traditional comics for kids

The *Beano* is one of Britain's longest running children's comics and its front cover demonstrates many of the codes and conventions we would expect to see in this genre. It targets a young audience with its bright, primary colours and large fonts, and features well-established, easily recognisable characters who conform to conventional stereotypes.

Most publications feature the price and a website address on the front page and that is the case with the front cover of the *Beano*, in **A**. There's also a masthead declaring the name of the publication toward the top of the page. The font may appear old-fashioned as it is one of the many very traditional aspects of the page. The illustrations, which appear to be in **frames** rather like a comic strip, give readers a taste of what to expect if they buy the comic.

Other comic book conventions are:

- onomatopoeic words (words that imitate the sound they are describing, e.g. crash, smash)
- movement lines to trace the movement of the wrecking ball or the water shooting from the water pistol
- stereotypical characters, such as the teacher in the bottom left-hand corner
- a slogan – 'menacingly funny'
- **lures** to encourage the readers, such as 'win'; or invitations to join the Beano Club.

In analysing a front cover like the *Beano's* you'd discuss the codes and conventions and use terms like 'slogan' and 'lure'. You might go on to discuss how the comic appeals to its audience, the stereotypical characters and the narrative.

Objectives

To learn about the codes and conventions and some technical terms that apply to the front covers of comics.

A *A front cover of the* Beano

Key terms

Frames: the boxes or shapes in which the text and drawings of the comic appear.

Lures: attempts to attract the audience or reader by offering something.

Anti-hero: usually the main character who the audience cheer on but who has a number of negative characteristics.

Comics for older kids

Comics that target an older audience tend to feature a striking single image to attract the reader's attention. Comics such as *2000AD* (**B**) show iconic **anti-hero** Judge Dredd assaulting two criminals, one who appears 'alien'. Like many comics aimed at an older reader, Dredd is a character who saves the day and restores law and order. He's not entirely a super-hero but there are similarities with Superman, Spiderman and lots of other comic book heroes. In analysing a cover from a comic of this type, you would again focus on the typical codes and conventions and refer to key terms. Representation, narrative and audience appeal could all be discussed in detail.

Activity

Comics often offer a free gift in the form of a covermount to entice readers. What might be given away with the *Beano* or *2000AD*? Research this further by looking at the comics in your local supermarket or newsagent.

B 2000AD, *home of Judge Dredd and his nemesis the Warlock*

C *An example of a student's work: a hand-drawn front cover for a comic*

Later on in this section there is guidance on how to produce your own creative work on magazines but, as we're on the subject of comics, it's useful to look at an example of a student's work in **C**.

This is a successful attempt at designing and presenting a new comic on the part of the student because:

- A number of codes and conventions are evident.
- There is enough colour and sense of narrative to appeal to a potential audience.

Assessment – Grade B.

AQA *Examiner's tip*

If you choose to present material for a new magazine you'll be expected to include photographs, but working on a comic does allow you to submit hand-drawn material because this is appropriate to the medium of comics. It would probably be wise to use some computer-generated text as part of the cover.

2.7 Controlled assessment: Assignment 1

Introduction

As part of AQA GCSE media studies, and having studied the front covers of magazines or comics, it's time to turn your attention to the controlled assessment. For assignment 1, you are required to analyse two popular magazine or comic front covers, and to discuss how they appeal to their target audience. You cannot mix magazines and comics here – you have to analyse and discuss the front covers of two magazines or two comics.

Your response needs to be approximately 400 words.

Objectives

To plan and produce your analysis of two popular magazine or comic front covers.

Analysing magazine and comic front covers

Step 1

- What is the name of each magazine or comic you have chosen to analyse?
- What type is each magazine/comic?
- How is the name of each magazine/comic appropriate or appealing?
- Examine the mastheads. What are the connotations of the mastheads?
- If there is a logo, what does this tell you about the identity of the magazines/comics?
- Comment on the colours, fonts, position and size of the mastheads.

Step 2

- Look at the main image. How has it been used on each front cover?
- Who is in the main image? Why have they been chosen?
- Comment on the facial expression, clothes, jewellery, direct or indirect address, pose and positioning of the main person featured on the cover of each magazine/comic.
- What is the impact of the cover image on each magazine's/comic's target audience?
- How have captions been used to anchor the image?

Step 3

- Using the correct terminology, describe the layout and style of each front cover.
- How has colour been used?
- What is the overall impact of the layout, colour and style? How would it appeal to the target audience?

Step 4

- Focus on the sell lines. How are they appropriate and how do they attract the audience?
- How is language used in the headlines and text? How would it appeal to the target audience?
- What type of articles are featured on the covers? How would they attract the target audience?
- Describe any offers or enticements on the covers. How do they appeal to the target audience?

Step 5

- Who is the target audience for each publication?
- How might this audience use the text? (You might use Blumler and Katz's uses and gratifications theory to help you with this.)

Step 6

- What can you say about how people are represented by the front covers?

Step 7

- Overall, explain how each front cover is designed to appeal to the target audience.

What one student did

Analysis of magazines

The general nature of NME magazine is very serious and 'rock and roll'. The mode of address is on the level of the readers, casual and knowledgeable about the music industry. NME magazine sometimes use slang or swear words which don't offend or shock the readers. In this particular issue, a band called Oasis are featured on the front. This is likely because Oasis have just released a new album or making a comeback so therefore they want some publicity. NME itself will also gain some publicity for featuring a popular band such as Oasis. It's sort of a dual-promotion as both Oasis and NME will gain popularity. The size of the image of Oasis takes up the majority of the page which emphasises the importance and the large amounts of popularity the band have.

Both members of Oasis are giving direct address. This is because they want to look cool and serious. Direct address makes it seem more personal, as if Oasis is looking directly at the reader. Neither of the band members are smiling which reflects Oasis' attitude. One of the men are also wearing sunglasses, which adds to this. The colours of the page add to the serious impression created, as there are a lot of black and dark colours. The connotations of dark colours such as black are alarming, dangerous and mysterious, as well as serious.

There is a quote from Oasis including a swear word, which is blanked out by stars. This shows that Oasis will be giving there honest opinions in the magazine and fans of the band are going to want to know what they have to say. The swearing also fits in with the 'rebellious' image of both the band and the magazine.

A *A student's work for GCSE: a written analysis of* NME *magazine*

A is an extract of a media studies student's written analysis of *NME*. Notice that a number of technical terms have been used (connotation, direct address and mode of address) and that for all of these an explanation is offered of the effect they have. There are references to audience – who they might be and how the magazine attracts them. The handwritten comments on the right are from the teacher, who also uses underlining to show where the analysis is making good points. Remember that you have only 400 words in which to complete your analysis. One way of reducing the number of words would be to use bullet points or to annotate the text, like we did on pages 24–25 with *FourFourTwo* magazine.

AQA *Examiner's tip*

When analysing a media text, you need to go beyond describing what you see: you need to explain why it has been designed or written a certain way.

links

Refer back to pages 24–25 for the media terminology used to describe the layout and style of a front cover.

2.8 Presenting your own ideas

Get creative

Once you have completed your analytical work you'll need to begin the creative work on the same topic for the next part of your assessment. In the following topic is a step-by-step guide to this exercise, but here we'll look at some good examples of the sort of work you might produce.

Objectives

To learn from an example of creative work produced by a GCSE Media Studies student.

A *A student's work for GCSE: mock-up of a front cover for a rock magazine*

You need to produce a magazine front cover. The example in **A** is a very good one because it includes lots of relevant codes and conventions. It's easy to recognise the genre of the magazine and the cover has impact and appeal. You may submit this as a hand-drawn piece as this is a pre-production test. You may, however, wish to develop it further in order to enhance your skills.

Happy snapping

Once you have a good idea of what you want to do, you need to take the appropriate photographs. Here's a fabulous example from a 16-year-old GCSE media studies student.

B *A student's work for GCSE: a magazine front cover*

Main image

A superb original photograph identifies the target audience. There is direct address (the man is looking at the camera) and there's some degree of activity. It's very colourful and the flowers link to the Gardener's Guide which is free inside.

Sell lines

The font is suitably old-fashioned and the colours link with the flowers. There are six topics mentioned and all relate to the target audience. This demonstrates some research on the part of the student. There are rhetorical questions and buzz words like 'special' and 'free'.

In this instance the magazine is not aimed at the student or his or her friends. The vast majority of creative work by GCSE media studies students aims to appeal to a late-teen audience, so it is refreshing to see that this student has aimed at a different audience.

Assessment

This piece of student's work includes lots of magazine codes and conventions – masthead, bar code, price and date. It claims to be a 'summer issue' and it certainly looks like it is! It certainly meets a Level 6 description (the top level) – "There is flair and creativity. Material is presented skillfully." It has to be awarded a Grade A at GCSE.

2.9 Controlled assessment pre-production task

Introduction

As part of AQA GCSE media studies, students are required to:

...present a pre-production task. They will need to explain their intentions, with particular reference to their use of media language and how it will appeal to the target audience.

For your controlled assessment on magazines or comics you will need to design the front cover of a magazine or comic aimed at a specific audience.

You may discuss the work with others, but you are not allowed to submit work as a group. This is an individual assignment.

Step 1 Planning

- Decide the context and audience for your magazine or comic.
- Decide on the style and genre.
- Determine your potential audience.
- How are you going to design a front cover that will attract your audience?
- Record your decisions on a planning sheet.

Step 2 Design

- Decide on a title for your magazine or comic.
- Design a masthead and logo.

Step 3 Content

- What sort of articles are going to feature on your cover?
- What types of images are you going to include?
- How are you going to use colour on the front cover?

Step 4 Layout

- Draw a mock-up of your front cover. Use frames and boxes to indicate where different features will be placed.
- Decide which features to include.

Step 5 Production (Optional)

- If you choose to produce a final version of your front cover, include original text and photography where possible.

Step 6 Write up

- Explain how the layout and design of your front cover would attract your target audience. You might say something about how your magazine or comic represents the people featured on the cover.

Objectives

To learn how to approach the pre-production task.

Remember

The aim of a front cover is to grab the audience's attention. Your front cover needs to have impact.

links

You may wish to revisit pages 24–26 on the conventions used on front covers of magazines and comics.

What one student did

A *A student's work for GCSE:* Tattoo *magazine front cover*

An Examiner says:

In **A** we have the front cover of a magazine on tattoos, prepared by a GCSE media studies student. Most codes and conventions are evident: masthead, bar code, price and sell lines. The main image overlaps the masthead of the magazine, which is another typical feature. Interesting fonts are used and there's a colour scheme. Most striking is the original photograph, which addresses the audience appropriately in terms of the look, age and style of the model. The sell lines might have been arranged more carefully, but this piece of work would earn a high GCSE grade.

Summary

In this chapter, you have learned about:

- different genres of magazines and comics
- the key terms, and codes and conventions of front covers
- the layout of front covers
- how to analyse front covers using denotation and connotation
- audience profiles and how magazines target audiences
- how audiences use magazines and comics
- representation in magazines and comics
- how to approach the controlled assessment by analysing existing covers and then preparing your own.

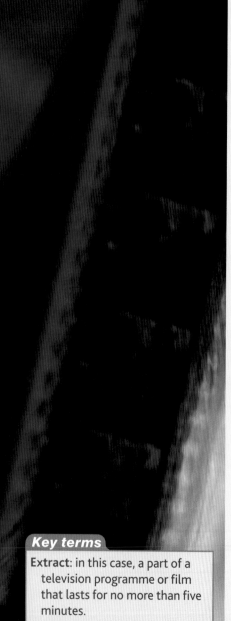

3 Moving image

Objectives

To learn about what is required for the analysis of a moving image text and about the codes and conventions of television situation comedies.

About this topic

What you will need to do

If you or your teacher chooses moving image for Assignment 1, you will be required to write about the opening five minutes of one television programme or feature film. To do this successfully, you will need to:

- Look at the extract closely, which will mean watching it several times, taking notes and discussing it with your teacher and class-mates.
- Analyse the **extract** closely, using media terminology and considering the way the film or television programme catches the attention of its audience.
- Focus purely on the extract you or your teacher chooses.

With only approximately 400 words in which to write your response, you should be careful not to just describe what you see. Analysis involves going into detail about particular features rather than 'summing up' the whole extract.

A breakdown of the tasks

Here's a useful breakdown of what you will be required to do.

- Write about the typical codes and conventions of the genre of the extract.
- Show understanding of aspects of media language.
- Use technical terms.
- Say something about representation.
- Consider the effect on the audience.

Following this you'll be asked to present ideas for a moving image piece of your own in the same genre. Using what you've learned about moving image texts and the genre you've studied, you will write a brief report (approximately 100 words) on your ideas.

Focusing on television

In this section, we will look at how to analyse the opening five minutes of a television programme. This will include the title sequence and the first scenes of the programme. In order to make this more manageable we are going to look at one particular genre – situation comedy, also known as **sitcom**.

First, complete the following starter activity.

Key terms

Extract: in this case, a part of a television programme or film that lasts for no more than five minutes.

Starter activity

Here are six popular television programmes. Only three of them are sitcoms. Which three?

A The Bill

B Holby City

C Everybody Hates Chris

D Skins

E Only Fools and Horses

F The Simpsons

In order to qualify as a sitcom, a programme will need to use typical generic codes and conventions. In other words, most sitcoms will follow a similar pattern or formula. If you said that what *The Simpsons* and *Only Fools and Horses* (which are both sitcoms) have in common is that they both:

1 have a theme tune
2 have a limited number of main characters who appear in every episode, and
3 last roughly 25 minutes

you'd be showing awareness of these typical generic codes and conventions.

Other programmes might have elements of the genre. *The Bill* may involve a small group of characters who are 'trapped' at Sun Hill police station, and there may be lots of hilarious events in *Skins*, but both programmes are much more about drama than comedy. Sitcoms aren't only about humour though. We often feel sorry for characters that we've grown to love, and some sitcoms can be quite emotional and dramatic.

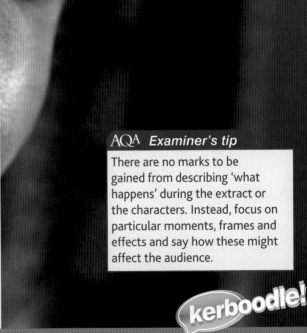

AQA *Examiner's tip*

There are no marks to be gained from describing 'what happens' during the extract or the characters. Instead, focus on particular moments, frames and effects and say how these might affect the audience.

kerboodle!

3.1 Pre-title sequences

Objectives

To learn about pre-title sequences and how they introduce audiences to a show.

To learn a number of key terms and how they apply to the codes and conventions of sitcoms.

Media brief

My Name is Earl

We are going to analyse some aspects of the opening sequences of one episode of US sitcom, *My Name is Earl*. This was first broadcast in the UK on Channel 4 in 2006.

A My Name is Earl *is produced by 20th Century Fox Television*

B *Earl with his brother Randy and ex-wife Joy*

My Name is Earl, from the second series, begins with a brief introduction to the show, a sort of pre-title sequence. This aims to reassure viewers that they are about to enjoy a typical episode of a favourite programme.

- All of the main characters appear to remind the audience of who they are and to offer reassurance that nothing has changed and that their favourite character will feature in this episode.
- The usual interactions will occur. From facial expressions, it's possible to identify some familiar character traits. Randy appears bemused. Joy is annoyed. Earl is thoughtful, as he considers how he will deal with another set of problems.

- The typical location of the Crab Shack, is used and the bar and all its furnishings, as well as the characters' clothing, all appear the same as in previous episodes. This further reinforces the idea that all is as it should be.

The sequence also serves as a taster: an attempt to hook the audience by introducing the story or narrative for this particular episode.

From the pre-title sequence, we can see a number of typical sitcom codes and conventions:

Setting

Most sitcoms are filmed indoors. This makes them cheaper to produce. The sets can be built in a television studio, which gives a controlled environment and these sets can be used repeatedly. There is no **fourth wall**.

Characters

A small group of main characters appears in every episode: Earl, Randy, Joy, Crabman and Catalina. Other characters appear in supporting roles. They appear quite often, but their importance is only seen in terms of how they affect the main characters. For instance, Patty, the daytime hooker, appears in a number of episodes but only when she crosses paths with Earl.

Lighting

While supposedly 'realistic' or (as media people prefer!) naturalistic lighting is often **high key** and quite bright so the show will appear more colourful than in real life. This will not only be so that the audience can clearly see what is happening, but is also likely to make the appearance of the show more attractive.

Mise-en-scène

As with lighting, the way the characters are dressed, the décor and furnishings (the props) will all appear realistic. In many sitcoms, *Sex and the City* for instance, clothes and surroundings may appear quite glamorous, more attractive than 'real life'. However, Earl's world is not glamorous!

Editing

Continuity editing is used, which means that the editing of shots will seem to naturally follow the progress of a particular scene. Editors working in other genres might be more ambitious and daring.

Camera work

Again, in sitcoms, this tends to be fairly conventional following the dialogue. Most scenes begin with an **establishing shot**. The scene begins with a medium or long shot to show us which characters are involved and what they are doing. Most of the shots in a sitcom will be medium shots, as the main need is to tell the story and allow the audience to understand the dialogue. *My Name is Earl*, like *Scrubs*, does include some more adventurous uses of the camera.

Activity

We say that we 'watch' a television programme but we also hear it. There is dialogue (or speech), incidental music and sound effects. In many sitcoms (but not *My Name is Earl*) there may be audience laughter. What effect on viewers would these sound features have?

The dialogue will try to entertain viewers by ...

Incidental music is added because ...

Audience laughter is used to ...

Key terms

Fourth wall: when filmed in a TV studio, a sitcom will usually only show three walls. For instance, in *Friends*, when the Central Perk set is used, the camera (and therefore the audience) will always occupy the fourth wall.

High key: very bright lighting which creates a glossy look that can give a glamorous feel but may seem artificial.

Establishing shot: to show the audience a change of location, a still shot of the exterior of a location will be shown.

links

See pages 10–11 for information on different shot types.

3.2 Title sequences

The Friends title sequence

Some title sequences become very famous and stay largely the same in order to remind the viewers of the programme they've grown to love, and to present a cheerful and positive impression of the show.

By the time you've done the group activity, you should have plenty to say about the *Friends* title sequence – and much of this could be applied to other opening title sequences where the aim is to introduce the sitcom. All aspects of the title sequence are basically there for the same reason – to encourage the audience to watch the programme.

Did you say anything about:

- the font used for presenting the word 'Friends'
- the location
- dancing?

The font

This can be described as informal or even cheerful, as if it's been handwritten by someone who is confident and in a good mood! There are also coloured dots in between the white letters, which correspond to the colours of the umbrellas. These are primary colours and have connotations of fun and happiness.

A *Repeats of* Friends *are shown regularly on E4*

Objectives

To learn about title sequences and how to apply media terms when analysing them.

Group activity

As a class, view the title sequence of an episode of *Friends*. Now work with three class mates and write down five things that you notice about the title sequence. In order to avoid everyone listing the most obvious aspects, you will score one point for each thing you notice but three points if no other group has noticed the same thing. Up to three more points can be scored for an explanation of *why* this item was included in the sequence.

Example: All of the cast are seen with umbrellas.

Reason: The umbrellas are very colourful and seem almost like toys. This makes the sequence look more fun.

It is up to your teacher to decide whether this and any other 'reason' is worth one, two or three points.

The location

The location is a fountain in Central Park, New York City. It is an exciting and glamorous city, but sometimes associated with crime. But here the characters are in the park and there's no sense of danger. The fountain suggests the culture of the city but offers an excuse for childish play.

Dancing

The denotation is moving bodies in time to music; the connotation is having fun, feeling happy and confident.

Whether it's because the characters are attractive and appealing or whether it's because there are a lot of rapid **cuts** from shot to shot to suggest excitement, the aim of the title sequence is to make the show look (and sound) as attractive as possible.

Theme tunes

The *Friends* title sequence is accompanied by a theme tune, 'I'll be there for you' by the Rembrandts. This is cheerful pop rock for young adults and is appropriate to the target audience of mainly middle-class college students (past, present or future). This isn't to say that other groups of people can't watch *Friends* or listen to the Rembrandts, but there is a core audience that can be identified.

Think about how the theme tune for other sitcoms seems to fit the programme. The very well-known theme tunes for *The Fresh Prince of Bel Air* and *Only Fools and Horses* are good examples of how music is chosen to give a flavour of the programme and the expected audience it will attract.

B *The Rembrandts*

Key terms

Cut: an immediate change from one image to another.

Extension activity

Write between 100 and 200 words explaining how the opening sequence to *Friends* (or one other sitcom) is appropriate for the programme and would be attractive and appealing to its core audience.

links

Refer back to pages 10–11 on media language.

3.3 Audience and situation comedy

The ritual pleasure of consuming something familiar

One aspect of long-running television series that helps to make them popular is familiarity. If an audience becomes familiar with the characters and settings, they may be more inclined to return for repeated viewings. This partly accounts for the appeal of soap operas by audiences and producers alike. Audiences are attracted by the familiar; producers are happy to provide what they think an audience wants.

Sitcoms meet the genre requirement of giving audiences what they want. The format, the characters and the settings will rarely change. The theme music will always be the same too. Does this make sitcoms boring?

The writers will try to surprise us with the plots and the dialogue but within certain limitations. For instance, anything can happen to the characters but none of them will die (apart from Kenny in *South Park* – and even he will reappear in the next episode!). We know that whatever disruption occurs, by the end, normality (or equilibrium) will be restored.

Mainstream

Sitcoms like *Friends*, *My Family* and *Only Fools and Horses* can be described as mainstream, because they appeal to massive audiences and appear on the most watched television channels at peak viewing times. They may vary in many ways, but they share the most common sitcom conventions and can be described as 'conventional'.

Niche

There are other sitcoms, such as *Curb Your Enthusiasm*, *Two Pints of Lager and a Packet of Crisps* and *Family Guy,* which for various reasons are not mainstream or conventional. They appear on less popular channels and attract smaller but often dedicated audiences. These 'cult' sitcoms use many of the genre conventions we are used to, but often change them or make fun of them.

Applying Blumler and Katz's theory

Which of Blumler and Katz's reasons for people consuming media texts apply to sitcoms? For this exercise we'll look at *Everybody Hates Chris*, but any sitcom could be tested against their theory.

To inform/educate

Sitcoms don't usually set out to inform or educate an audience. However, *Everybody Hates Chris* is set in 1970s America and social issues feature strongly, so we are informed about how life might have been for Afro-Americans at the time. It's not exactly factual, but we do learn something.

Objectives

- To learn how sitcoms appeal to particular audiences.
- To learn how to apply Blumler and Katz's theory to a sitcom.

A *Kenny from* South Park *dies in every episode – the audience knows to expect this*

Did you know ??????

Blumler and Katz suggested the following reasons for people consuming media texts: for information/education; for entertainment; for social interaction; for 'escape'; for the identity they offer.

To entertain

Everybody Hates Chris entertains by making us laugh and by ending on a happy note to leave us with a feel-good factor.

For social interaction

Social interaction is a factor because *Everybody Hates Chris* is the sort of programme that you can watch with friends and family, and it's definitely one that viewers will bring up in conversation. ('Did you see…?')

To escape

Everybody Hates Chris is not the most taxing viewing, so it helps us to relax. While some of the problems encountered by the chracters are ones that we might one day face, they are never presented as a cause for doom and gloom!

Identification

While the show is set in the US, the lifestyle of the characters is something that viewers can relate to. Everyone has felt badly treated at times and so can relate to Chris. Older viewers might identify with one of his parents.

B *Why do you watch sitcoms such as* Everybody Hates Chris?

Activity

1 Apply Blumler and Katz's theory to a sitcom such as *Friends* or *My Name is Earl*, or to your own favourite sitcom. Use the *Everybody Hates Chris* example to help you copy and complete the following:

a [Name of sitcom] informs and educates us by showing …

b [Name of sitcom] is entertaining because …

c [Name of sitcom] allows for social interaction as …

d Viewers can feel a sense of escape when watching … because …

e The audience can relate to some of the characters and situations which gives them identification. Examples of this are …

links

Refer back to the topic of audience on pages 12–13.

kerboodle!

3.4 Niche audiences

Case study

The Mighty Boosh

The Mighty Boosh first appeared on radio and then on television, on BBC3, in 2004. It has grown in popularity and the third series was 'promoted' to BBC2. But the true measures of the show's appeal are the sell-out live shows at theatres and arenas across the UK, healthy sales of DVD box sets and frequent sightings of the *Boosh* logo on T-shirts and other merchandise. Looking at the still here and from viewing extracts from the programme, you can perhaps see how 'different' *The Mighty Boosh* is from mainstream sitcoms.

A The Mighty Boosh *on their 2008 tour*

Objectives

To learn about niche audiences and how to construct an audience profile for a sitcom.

Key terms

Rupture of verisimilitude: verisimilitude means the attempt by film-makers to show reality or normality. This is ruptured (or broken) when something clearly unrealistic happens. Talking directly to the viewers would be an example of this.

Cult: a group of devoted followers that sets itself apart from a main group.

Activity

Here are 10 things I noticed in one episode of *The Mighty Boosh*. Five of them could happen in other sitcoms, but five are unusual for this genre. Try to work out which five are mainstream or conventional and which five are more unusual and suited to a programme appealing to a niche audience.

- Each episode of a series is set in the same location.
- The characters will often talk directly to the camera/audience (**rupture of verisimilitude**).
- Each episode ends with a song.
- Lighting and camera effects are often used to create a strange atmosphere.
- Catchphrases are used, e.g. 'It's an outrage!'
- One of the characters is a gorilla – Bolo. He talks and works as a DJ.
- There are five main characters that appear in every episode.
- The two main characters seem to be in competition with one another.
- Every episode involves a narrative or story which is resolved by the end.
- The moon appears in many episodes. It has a face and talks to the viewers.

Who is into *The Mighty Boosh*?

So, if *The Mighty Boosh* is an example of a programme that appeals to a niche or **cult** audience – who would make up this audience? It's always difficult to pin down an audience exactly, but we can try and identify a core audience.

It's pretty obvious that *The Mighty Boosh* is 'strange', so it would appeal to people who are into surreal stuff. The characters don't dress in a 'normal' way so it's possible that the audience won't be people who dress in a conventional way. The programme tends to break sitcom conventions, so it might appeal to people who go against conventions.

If you were to attend *The Mighty Boosh* live show you'd have an even better insight. Of the 5000 people who attended the Nottingham Arena shows, in November 2008, the vast majority were white and aged between 15 and 25. Probably two-thirds were female and many were dressed in black with an inclination toward the goth/emo look. It would be fair to assume that many of them would read the *NME* or *Kerrang!* and would be in further education (students) or would have left further education in recent years. This might place them in the B–C1 bracket. Older audience members were perhaps teachers of English, Drama, Dance or Media Studies.

In conclusion, *The Mighty Boosh* audience seems to be made up of unconventional, rebellious types. Or at least that's how they like to be seen! They are mainly young and female. They are artistic, student types who like to be into something different from the mainstream.

AQA Examiner's tip

Many students new to media studies assume that newspapers, films, songs and so on are aimed at everybody, or that if they don't like something no one will. They couldn't be more wrong! Remember – whoever you are, *most* people are different from you!

Extension activity

Construct an audience profile for a different sitcom.

- Choose a sitcom.
- Decide whether it's a mainstream or cult sitcom.
- When and where (on what channel) is it broadcast?
- Consider the age, gender, ethnicity and lifestyle of the main characters.
- Take into account whether there is any bad language or adult content.
- Find out who watches the programme from your friends, family, teachers and anyone else you can ask.
- Take into account their age, gender, ethnic make-up, occupation and lifestyle.

From the above you should have a reasonable chance of constructing an audience profile!

links

Look at audience on pages 12–13 and at the reader profiles for magazines on pages 28–29.

kerboodle!

3.5 Narrative and representation in sitcoms

Todorov

The narrative or story of a sitcom often follows a particular pattern which fits the narrative theory of Tzetan Todorov, a Bulgarian philosopher. According to Todorov, narratives begin with an equilibrium where everything might be calm or settled (Once upon a time ...), but the story is then propelled by a disruption. Characters then attempt to correct the situation and eventually everything returns to something like normal – the resolution (They all lived happily ever after.) This formula is particularly appropriate with sitcoms, where a 30-minute format in which the main situation cannot change is quite restrictive.

Briefly, Todorov's narrative theory can be remembered as:

Equilibrium – disruption – struggle to repair disruption – resolution

In your five-minute extract it's unlikely that there'll be more than the first two stages.

Complications

1. Not all sitcoms follow a **linear narrative**. Flashbacks are often used – such as in *My Name is Earl*. Sometimes the same story might be told from different points of view, giving a rather fragmented narrative.
2. Sometimes more than one storyline might feature in a single episode. This is often the case for *Scrubs* or *Friends*, where a number of stories involve different main characters. In *Malcolm in the Middle*, for example, eldest brother Francis lives away from the main family group. His adventures form a **sub-plot**.

Propp

Another useful theory is that of Vladimir Propp, a Russian critic who identified a number of character types in folk tales. These can usually be seen in modern media texts. Sometimes films or television programmes will play with audience expectations, but usually you can clearly identify Propp's character types.

Hero – princess – villain – donor or mentor – helper

Again, in a five-minute extract you might not see all of these character types. However, many familiar programmes can be quickly viewed in terms of Propp's theory. For instance, in some episodes of *The Simpsons*, Homer will be the hero, Marge the princess, Mr Burns the villain and other characters would act as donors/mentors or helpers.

Objectives

To learn about narrative and representation in sitcoms.

Key terms

Linear narrative: a storyline that progresses in chronological order from beginning to end.

Sub-plot: a less important story than the main plot.

Stereotyping: the portrayal of people or places through a few obvious characteristics.

A Scrubs: *who is the hero, the princess, the villain, and the helper or donor?*

Representation in sitcoms

Referring to representation is going beyond the expectations of this, your first media assignment. Any discussion of this issue should earn you extra marks.

You might comment on **stereotypes**. Comedies usually deal with exaggerated characters who we can easily recognise. In *The Simpsons* you could say that Bart fits the stereotype of a naughty school boy, while Lisa is a typical clever, hard-working school girl. Catherine Tate's character, Lauren, and *Little Britain's* Vicky Pollard seem to have helped to create a stereotype of teenage girls.

It would be even more impressive if you were to consider the *effect* of stereotypes. A problem with stereotyping can be that people start to believe often negative portrayals. For instance, blondes really are dumb. Looking at the example from *The Simpsons*, you could say that the gender stereotyping of Bart and Lisa (and perhaps Homer and Marge) encourages people to behave in a similar way. Another effect might be that people begin to think that most teenage girls are like Lauren or Vicky Pollard.

You might even think about the impression viewers might get of a place or a group of people from the way they are presented in the sitcom. If you watched *Friends* and *My Name is Earl*, you'd get very different impressions of life in America.

B The Royale Family: *are there any stereotypical characters here? What impression of the British or of people who live in the north of England might viewers get from this programme?*

Activities

1. a Choose any one episode of a sitcom. Apply Todorov's narrative theory to the main plot.

   b Identify the main character types according to Propp's theory.

2. Think of a sitcom that you know well.

   a Try to spot any stereotypical characters.

   b Consider whether these stereotypes might influence viewers.

   c Think about the images or impressions someone might get from a sitcom.

AQA *Examiner's tip*

Remember to talk in terms of narrative structure and character types when you plan your own creative responses for Assignment 1. You might refer to Todorov and Propp for extra credit!

kerboodle!

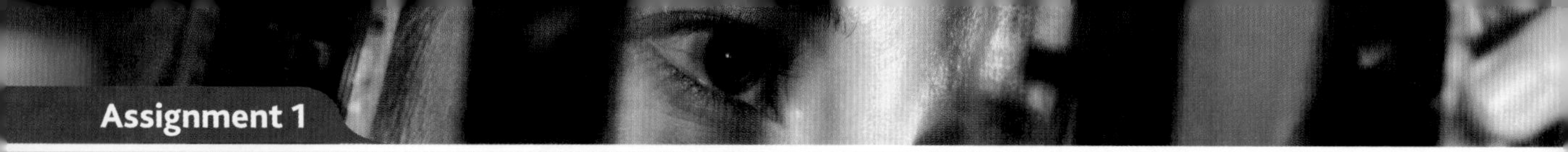

3.6 Controlled assessment: Assignment 1

Introduction

As part of AQA GCSE media studies, and having studied moving image through the genre of television sitcom, you need to begin planning your work for Assignment 1 of the controlled assessment. You are required to analyse the opening five minutes of a film or television programme and discuss how the film or programme appeals to its target audience. Your response needs to be approximately 400 words.

Analysing moving image extracts

Step 1

- Look in detail at the pre-title sequence and the opening title sequence. Comment on how they try to appeal to the audience.
- Try to use media terms and media language: denotation and connotation; long-shot, close-up, *mise-en-scène*, high key lighting, etc.
- Recognise typical genre codes and conventions and, if appropriate, where these are broken.

Step 2

- Think about the audience for the film or television programme. Can you apply some aspects of Blumler and Katz's theory to explain why an audience might watch?
- Is the film or television programme mainstream or niche in its audience appeal?
- Think about the potential core audience. Try to construct an audience profile.

Step 3

- What clues are offered in your chosen extract about the narrative structure?

Step 4

- Can you say anything about how the film or television programme represents people or places? Does it give positive or negative presentations? Are stereotypes used?

Objectives

To plan and produce your analysis of a five-minute extract of a moving image text.

AQA Examiner's tip

In order to stay within word limits, it's acceptable to use bullet points or headings to present your work more effectively.

Remember

- You don't have to analyse a sitcom. All the topics covered in this chapter can be applied to a different television genre or to a film.
- You are only looking at a five-minute extract and the idea is to go into detail. Focus on particular moments or even individual shots. Don't try to explain everything, such as the story and who the characters are.

Student's Work – Analysis of the opening scenes of an episode of Father Ted

The TITLE SEQUENCE begins with shots of the scenery where the series takes place – 'Craggy Island'.

These shots are probably taken from an aeroplane or helicopter & remind me of Emmerdale.

These are all LONG SHOTS or ESTABLISHING SHOTS as they show where the action will take place.

MUSIC – the music sounds old fashioned and slightly comical. There are no lyrics but you get the idea that the music is meant to be funny.

TITLE – the name of the programme appears and an old-fashioned religious looking FONT is used which fits in with the idea that the programme features a priest. The letters are very large to show that Father Ted is an important man in the show. Even so, it's kind of funny that his name is large and 'important' as most of the time Ted is seen as foolish.

As the titles (actor's names) continues we see more of the island perhaps as if the plane or helicopter is coming to land. These are POINT OF VIEW shots showing what the pilot might see.

A house is seen and this will be a main setting. We can see it's in a very quiet area. Outside some characters are waving but they seem to leap out of the way as the camera getts nearer. SOUND EFFECTS are used – a propeller sound & a screeching noise to indicate that there's going to be a crash & then there's an explosion!

We see the three main characters getting out of the way. The picture goes blurry and disappears which is meant to show the crash.

EFFECT OF THE TITLE SEQUENCE

Shows the setting
Quick view of main characters
The crash & the music suggest that it's going to be a comedy.

Examiner's Commentary

Some of this is rather descriptive and it might have been a good idea not to describe every part of the opening sequence. However, there are technical terms used (in capital letters) and the response clearly indicates how the title sequence introduces the show as a comedy. The student can now go on to write about the next scenes as the show begins – and has about 200 more words left! So far this is a good-quality analysis which uses technical terms with confidence and looks likely to earn 8 marks of the 10 available for this task. There would need to be more discussion of audience before this could move into the top band of the mark scheme.

A *Construct an audience profile for your film or television programme*

3.7 Presenting your own ideas

Once you have completed your analytical work you'll need to begin the creative work on the same topic for the next part of your assessment. In the following topic is a step-by-step guide to this exercise, but here we'll look at a very good example of the sort of work you might produce.

Objectives

To learn from an excellent example of creative work produced by a GCSE Media Studies student.

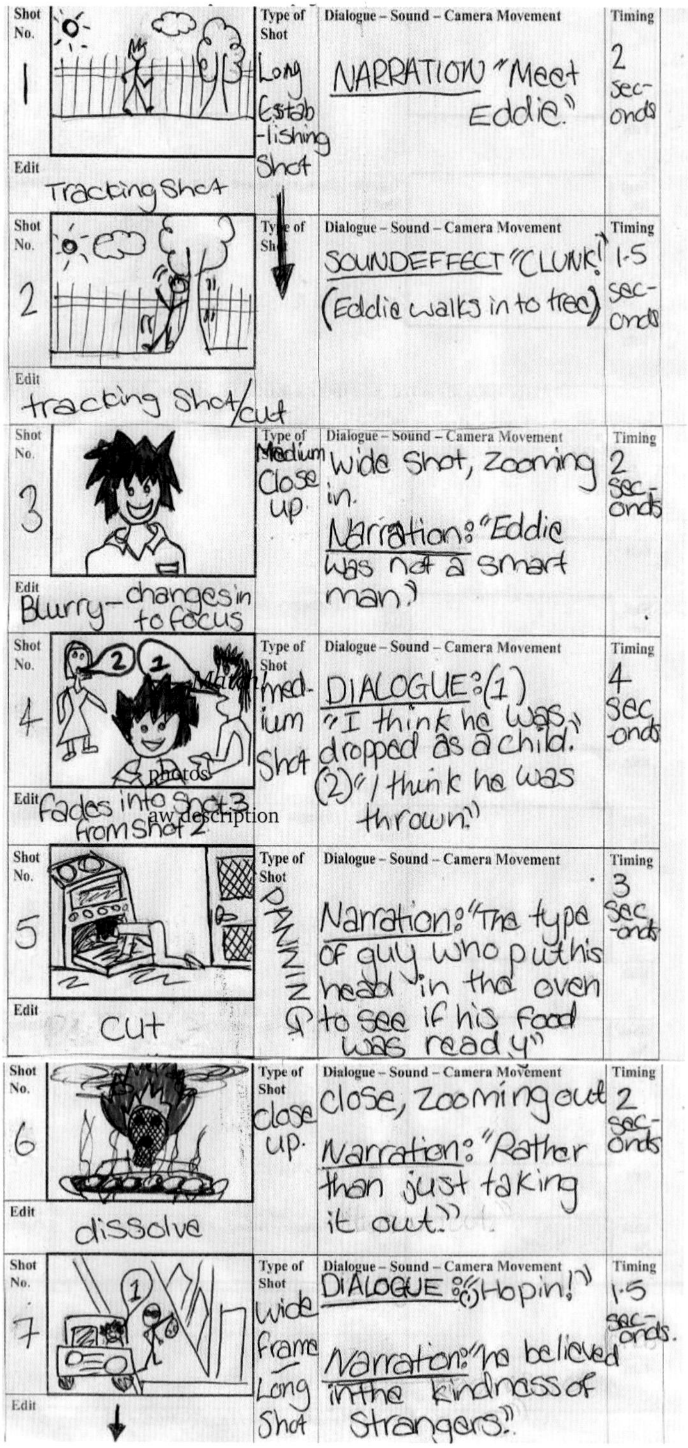

Shot No.	Edit	Type of Shot	Dialogue – Sound – Camera Movement	Timing
1	Tracking Shot	Long Establishing Shot	NARRATION "Meet Eddie."	2 seconds
2	tracking shot/cut	↓	SOUNDEFFECT "CLUNK!" (Eddie walks in to tree)	1.5 seconds
3	Blurry – changes in to focus	Medium Close up.	wide shot, Zooming in. Narration: "Eddie was not a smart man."	2 seconds
4	Fades into Shot 3 from shot 2	medium Shot	DIALOGUE: (1) "I think he was dropped as a child." (2) "I think he was thrown."	4 seconds
5	cut	PANNING	Narration: "The type of guy who put his head in the oven to see if his food was ready"	3 seconds
6	dissolve	close up.	close, Zooming out. Narration: "Rather than just taking it out."	2 seconds
7	↓	wide frame Long Shot	DIALOGUE (1): "Hopin!" Narration: "he believed in the kindness of Strangers."	1.5 seconds.

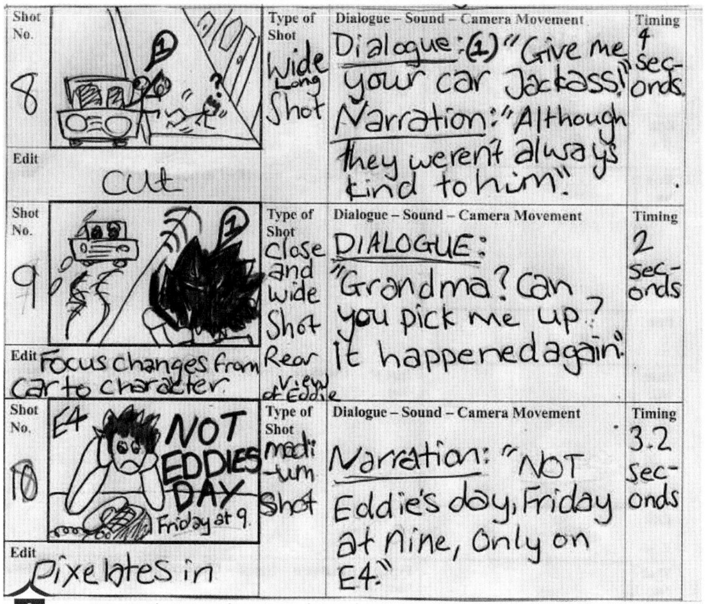

A *GCSE student work: a storyboard*

An examiner says

Dialogue 1 and 2 identify the two different speakers in this frame.

A good range of shot types, camera movements and edits are used.

Notice that the timings are quite short. The longest that any shot is on screen is four seconds. In total there are 25.2 seconds of material – an ample length for an opening sequence.

In some shots it's difficult to tell who 'Eddie' is – but his brightly coloured hair helps and for one frame we're told, 'Rear view of Eddie'.

Oops! There is narration and dialogue, but there is no music or sound effects! It's very likely that a television programme, especially a sitcom, would have music when it begins, so this work might lose marks as a result.

Grade

Despite the lack of music to accompany the sequence, there are many good ideas here. It's simply but clearly presented, with a clear sense of narrative. It's worth a Grade A.

Summary

The main strengths of this piece of work are that it clearly shows genre codes and conventions (character, humour, suggestions of narrative, narration) and it has a number of funny moments that would surely interest an audience if this were a real programme. There is a good range of shots and edits, and it succeeds in introducing the programme.

AQA Examiner's tip

What you can't show in the drawing, you can explain in writing.

Notice in **A** that for some shots the student has used stickmen drawings. Even so, it's possible to give a clear sense of what is happening. You don't have to be great at drawing, as long as you present your ideas simply and effectively.

Activity

Think of the type of music that might accompany this sequence. Write a description of it. What sort of instruments would be used? What mood would you be looking to create?

links

Compare this storyboard with the professionally produced storyboard on page 145.

3.8 Controlled assessment pre-production task

Introduction

As part of AQA GCSE Media Studies, students are required to:

...present a pre-production task. They will need to explain their intentions, with particular reference to their use of media language and how it will appeal to the target audience.

For your controlled assessment on moving image texts, you will need to design the opening of a film or television programme in the same genre as your analytical task, aimed at a specific audience.

The following activity is suitable for small group work.

Ideas can be submitted in the form of a script for the opening or most dramatic scenes, or as a storyboard using drawings, writing or photographs to represent what is seen on screen.

Step 1 Planning

Remind yourself of the genre you have studied and consider the main codes and conventions. Decide whether you will prepare a script or storyboard. You will need to have a clear idea of the film or television programme before you start, including the:

- title
- characters
- story outline
- settings and locations.

Record your decisions on a planning sheet.

Step 2 Thinking about the opening

You aren't required to produce the whole film or television programme, so think about how the opening can set the scene and introduce a character or characters. How will you introduce the narrative (equilibrium and disruption)? How will you interest and involve the audience?

Step 3 Presenting your ideas effectively

As a rough guide, 12 frames of a storyboard should be enough to introduce your film or television programme. A script should be no more than two sides of A4.

Both scripts and storyboards need to create an atmosphere by giving details about setting and location. Both need to use media terminology in describing camera shots and camera movement, lighting, *mise-en-scène* and editing. Your work should show evidence of appropriate genre codes and conventions.

Step 4 Write up

Explain, briefly:

- how your ideas demonstrate your knowledge of the genre
- how and why your ideas would appeal to an audience (and who that audience might be)
- how your ideas introduce the narrative.

Objectives

To learn how to approach the pre-production task.

Remember

The aim of the opening of a film or television programme is to grab the audience's attention. Your opening sequence needs to have impact.

AQA Examiner's tip

When you were analysing moving image texts you were told not to tell the story of the extract. The same applies here. Don't try to tell the whole story, instead give a flavour of your film or television programme. It doesn't matter if the audience don't know everything – they would find out more later if they watched the film or programme.

Refer to examples of story boards on pages 54–55 and 144–45 to help you with your own story board.

For 'Edit' you might write:

Cut: where one shot changes to another (the most common type of edit).

Dissolve: one shot slowly changes into the next (likely to be used for slower, atmospheric pieces)

Wipe: the edge of one shot slides off-screen to be replaced by the next.

Fade: Like a dissolve but here the shot disappears to leave a blank screen.

These edits or 'transitions' can be seen on Windows Movie Maker (see pages 146–147).

No.

STORYBOARD SHEET

Shot No.		Type of Shot	Dialogue – Sound – Camera Movement	Timing
Edit				
Shot No.		Type of Shot	Dialogue – Sound – Camera Movement	Timing
Edit				
Shot No.		Type of Shot	Dialogue – Sound – Camera Movement	Timing
Edit				
Shot No.		Type of Shot	Dialogue – Sound – Camera Movement	Timing
Edit				
Shot No.		Type of Shot	Dialogue – Sound – Camera Movement	Timing
Edit				

Summary

In this chapter you have learned about:

- different genres
- the key terms and codes and conventions
- pre-title and title sequences
- target audiences (niche and mainstream appeal)
- audience uses (using Blumler and Katz's theory)
- narrative theory
- representation
- how to approach the controlled assessment by analysing existing examples and then presenting ideas of your own.

4 Newspapers

Objectives

To learn about what is required for the analysis of newspaper front pages and to consider the importance of studying newspapers.

About this topic

What you will need to do

If you or your teacher selects the newspapers topic for Assignment 1, you will be required to write about two newspaper front pages. To do this successfully, you will need to look at the front pages closely and analyse their layout and the design. In your analysis, you need to use the correct media terminology and explain how each front page has been designed to attract the target audience of the newspaper. It is not necessary to compare the two pages. Your analysis needs to be approximately 500 words.

Things you need to know

Here's a useful list of topics you need to learn about that will help you complete Assignment 1:

- Learn about the different types of newspaper and their audience.
- Learn about the typical codes and conventions of front pages.
- Learn the correct media terminology for describing a front page.
- Understand how different newspapers target different audiences with their front pages.
- Understand how and why newspapers choose to report different news stories.

Following this you'll be asked to produce a newspaper front page of your own, designed to appeal to a specific audience. Then, using what you've learned about newspapers, you will need to write a brief report (no more than 100 words) on your ideas.

Why is the news important?

The news is any information about current events. It can be found in all channels of the media. But the news we hear is the end product of a process of selection and interpretation by media institutions. This makes the news media particularly powerful and influential. The news informs us about the world we live in; it shapes our understanding of events and it influences our opinions. It is a major media industry with a huge global audience. News is everywhere.

Starter activity

- List five current stories in the news.
- How did you hear about these news stories?
- Why do you think the media chose to report those stories?

> *"News is what somebody somewhere wants to suppress; all the rest is advertising."*
>
> *Lord Northcliffe – the owner of a number of UK newspapers*

A free press

In certain countries, media industries are controlled by the Government. These governments sometimes try to influence people's thoughts and actions by controlling what they hear from the media. Britain has a 'free press', which means that it is free of government control and can decide which stories to report on, and how it wishes to report them. Recent research suggests that more than a third of the world's population live in countries where there is no press freedom.

A *Demonstrating for a free press in Hungary, 20th September, 2006*

AQA Examiner's tip

A good analysis should identify the features of a media text and explain the purpose of those features.

4.1 UK newspapers

Newspaper sales

In the UK, newspapers have been around for over 300 years. Today they compete with other branches of the media, but before radio and television they were people's main source of information about what was happening.

While sales of newspapers have declined in recent years, however, they are still very popular, and millions of people regularly buy a daily paper.

Types of newspaper

The national UK daily newspapers are the most popular, but there are thousands of different newspapers published every week.

Regional newspapers: these include dailies such as the *Evening Standard* (London) and the *Daily Record* (Glasgow), and weeklies such as the *Cornish Guardian* and the *Herts and Essex Observer*

Sunday newspapers: these include the *News of the World*, the *Sunday Times* and the *Observer*, and regional Sunday papers such as the *Sunday Sun* (the North East)

Newspapers

Specialist newspapers: such as the *Asian Times* (ethnic), the *Methodist Recorder* (religion) and the *Racing Post* (horse racing)

The national dailies see table A

B *Types of newspaper*

Activities

Conduct a survey of newspaper readership in your class:

1. How popular are the national dailies in your class?
2. What other newspapers are bought by households from your class?
3. How many students read the newspapers?

Objectives

To examine the different kinds of newspaper available in the UK.

The net circulation of daily newspapers, 28 July to 24 August 2008

A *Source: ABC*

Name of newspaper	Total
Sun	3148792
Daily Mail	2258843
Daily Mirror	1455270
Daily Telegraph	860298
Daily Star	751494
Daily Express	748664
The Times	612779
Financial Times	417570
Guardian	332587
Independent	230033

MP's plan for gypsies
onpage 7

Conman to pay back cash
onpage 4

Look for jobs online at
www.bedsonsunday.com

November 16, 2008
Issue number: 1646
www.bedsonsunday.com

BEDFORDSHIRE **onsunday**

REGIONAL NEWSPAPER OF THE YEAR

BOROUGH EDITION

Cash down the plughole

BY KEELEY KNOWLES
keeley.knowles@bedsonsunday.com

A FAMILY has been sharing baths for months as their water bills were so high.

They then discovered they had been paying for their neighbour's supply as well as their own for the past three years.

Iona Scarlett and her partner Robert Rudder, moved into the property on Grosvenor Street, Bedford, in 2005, and began paying around £30 a month to Anglian Water.

As time went on, the cost of their supply rose until they were paying in excess of £100 a month, more than double what they should have been paying.

Mrs Scarlett, 45, and her sons Levi, 10, and Shaquille, 9, live at the house with Mr Rudder.

Mrs Scarlett said: "We tried cutting back on the amount of water we were using by sharing baths and only using the washing machine once a week but the bills kept getting higher."

Anglian Water visited the home earlier this year to fix a pipe which was leaking and discovered the truth behind the soaring water bills.

Mrs Scarlett said: "The surveyor came around about four weeks ago and stopped the supply to our house but the meter was still moving every time that next door flushed a lavatory or used the taps.

"That's when they realised we were sharing a meter with the house next door."

Mr Rudder, 43, said: "All that time we thought it must have been gold coming out of the taps but we were in fact paying for the supply to next door.

"We have probably paid hundreds of pounds more than what we should have done."

New meters will be installed in both properties in January and the couple will be compensated for the overpayment.

After *Bedfordshire on Sunday* became involved, Anglian Water informed the family that their direct debit would be suspended until the installation of the new meter.

A spokesman for Anglian Water said: "It is rare, but this can happen from time to time.

"When we took over responsibility for water supplies in the area many years ago we would have been working to data supplied by the local authority, which had listed this property as single supply.

"Obviously it was not and the pipes serving it were the same as the neighbouring property.

"It was the leak that alerted us to the fact that a lot of water was being used by this property and the problem was further complicated because the meter was full of builders sand.

"When the new meter is installed we will monitor how much water is being used in the first few weeks and work out how much on average the customer is using. We will then back date this and work out how much needs to be paid back in compensation."

SPLASHING OUT: Iona Scarlett with sons Levi and Shaquille, whose baths in future will not be as costly

US-style police chiefs needed here says MP

FIRST we had directly-elected mayors, now an MP is calling for directly-elected police chiefs.

MP Nadine Dorries wants to abolish Bedfordshire Police Authority.

On Tuesday Mrs Dorries, MP for Mid Bedfordshire, was a co-sponsor of a Ten Minute Rule Bill in the House of Commons.

The Bill was moved by fellow Conservative Douglas Carswell MP and would replace police authorities with elected police commissioners.

Police authorities are the governing bodies of police forces, who oversee the budgets and strategic direction of police forces. They are not directly elected but include councillors and members of the public.

Late last year Bedfordshire Police Authority came in for criticism as the police force was judged to be the poorest in the country in some respects.

Mrs Dorries said:"I am delighted to be a co-sponsor to this Bill and believe the single most effective move that could be taken to reduce crime in Bedfordshire, would be the abolition of the police authority and its replacement with an elected Police Commissioner.

"For decades, the gap between the concerns of the public and the accountability and responsiveness of the police to those concerns has widened.

"The clear message from the letters, telephone calls and emails I receive from my constituents every week, is the complete breakdown in trust in our criminal justice system. I share the public's frustrations on this matter and agree with them wholeheartedly.

"We need a radical shake-up as to how we tackle crime in this country and the abolition of the current Police Authorities would be a vital first step in realigning the concerns of the public, with the priorities of

■ **continued on page two**

C *What is the name of your local newspaper?*

Newspaper formats

National daily newspapers have traditionally been divided into two main groups:

1 Tabloids or 'popular press': popular **tabloids** are known as 'the red tops' because of their red mastheads, e.g. the *Sun, Daily Star,* the *Daily Mirror*. Middle market tabloids include the *Daily Express* and the *Daily Mail*.

2 The **broadsheets** or 'quality press': for example, *The Times,* the *Independent,* the *Guardian,* the *Daily Telegraph,* the *Financial Times*. In recent years, several 'quality' papers have adopted the tabloid print format.

Key terms

Tabloid: a size of newspaper (43 cm × 28 cm approx.); tabloids are traditionally more sensationalist and less serious in their news coverage.

Broadsheet: printed in a large format (74 cm × 59 cm approx.); broadsheets are more serious and detailed in their news coverage.

4.2 The national daily newspapers

The popular press (tabloids)

The way a tabloid covers the news is very different from a broadsheet. Tabloids aim to make the news easy to read. Articles are generally quite short and pages often contain large, colourful photographs. Front pages regularly feature scandal and gossip stories and the content is frequently dominated by entertainment and celebrity 'news'. The *Daily Star* even calls itself 'the official *Big Brother* paper'. Large sport sections, television news and page three pin-ups are features of these papers. The few 'serious' news stories they do cover largely focus on events in Britain.

The middle-market tabloids contain less gossip and scandal, and include some serious news stories. They pitch their audience between the red tops and the broadsheets. While being generally less sensationalist in style, like the red tops, they often feature human interest and scare stories.

The quality press (broadsheets)

These papers contain longer, more detailed articles. They focus more on serious news, including politics and international stories. Often they appear plainer and use a smaller typeface. They cost more than the tabloids, have more pages and circulation figures are generally lower.

Objectives

To examine the differences between the 'popular' and the 'quality' press.

THE INDEPENDENT
THE GOLDEN GAMES
UNFORGETTABLE IMAGES OF THE 2008 OLYMPICS
PLUS ALL THE NEWS FROM THE FINAL DAY SPORT, PAGES 42-45
Over to you, Boris
London's Mayor accepts the challenge to better Beijing
Fantastic at 50 Madonna kicks off world tour
Will Hillary ruin his party?
PLUS .media

A Independent, *Monday 25 August 2008*

THE Sun
THIS PAPER COSTS JUST 30p
£9k for paedo agony of girl, 3
NEST STOP LONDON
40 PAGES OF SPORT
BECKS: I'LL COACH GB UTD
Olympic footie dream for 2012 games

B Sun, *Monday 25 August 2008*

GOLDEN WONDERS
FREE 8-PAGE OLYMPIC PICTURE SOUVENIR
Daily Mail
DON'T DROP THE BATON BORIS!
As the Olympic flag is passed to London Mayor, the challenge: how DO you follow brilliant Beijing?

C Daily Mail, *Monday 25 August 2008*

We're your OFFICIAL Big Brother paper
DAILY STAR
BECKS AND LEONA KICK OFF BRIT GAMES
PREMIER LEAGUE
Wigan 0 M City 3
Chelsea 1 W Ham 0
FREE INSIDE Britain's No1 footie pullout
BB NICOLE: COCAINE GAZZA AND ME
MORE SEXY PICS INSIDE
RIK'S GIRL TALKS ONLY TO THE STAR

D Daily Star, *Monday 25 August 2008*

Activities

Examine the four newspaper headlines:

1. Describe the way each newspaper presents the Olympic handover.
2. Explain why these newspapers have reported the same story in different ways.
3. How similar and different are the four headlines?
4. What do the front pages tell you about the audience of these newspapers?

Audience

As you have already seen, there are significant differences in circulation figures between the national dailies. The *Sun* is the country's most popular national paper, while the *Financial Times* is the least popular (see table **E**). Newspapers are not only in competition with each other, but they also face competition from other news media. To maximise circulation, newspapers carefully target different audiences. An obvious example is the *Daily Star* which uses sport and sex to target a young male audience. Table **E** is from the National Readership Survey, and it gives a detailed breakdown of newspaper readership.

E *Readership estimates of daily newspapers, July 2007–June 2008. Source: National Readership Survey*

Name of newspaper	Total 000	ABC1 000	C2DE 000	15-24 000	45+ 000	Men 000	Women 000
Daily Express	1598	973	625	419	1179	820	778
Daily Mirror	3685	1514	2170	1526	2159	2087	1598
Daily Star	1484	398	1086	997	487	1057	427
Financial Times	377	354	23	214	163	286	91
Daily Mail	5347	3479	1867	1514	3833	2551	2795
Daily Telegraph	2060	1775	286	510	1551	1148	913
Guardian	1165	1061	105	620	545	641	524
Independent	702	619	83	362	340	423	279
Sun	8031	3009	5022	4600	3431	4527	3504
The Times	1731	1527	204	710	1022	1011	720

Activities

Look at table **E**:

5 What does the table tell you about the popularity of the quality and popular press?

6 How different is the readership between ABC1 and C2DE groups?

7 What does the table tell you about age and newspaper readership?

8 What does the table tell you about gender and newspaper readership?

4.3 The front page

Introduction

The front page is the most important page of a newspaper. It is the 'shop window' of a newspaper, designed to grab attention and sell the paper to the public. Front pages reinforce the newspaper's identity and project the paper's attitude to the events of the previous day. While the front pages of popular and quality newspapers may vary in content and style, both contain certain common conventions.

The design and layout of a front page is crucial. After the headlines have been created, the copy is written, and the photographs selected and sub-editors use computer technology to create the front page. Below is a front page from the *Daily Express*. The key terms indicate the layout of the page.

> **Objectives**
>
> To look at the layout and conventions of newspaper front pages.

DAILY EXPRESS

www.express.co.uk THE WORLD'S GREATEST NEWSPAPER WEDNESDAY OCTOBER 1, 2008 40p

STILL ONLY 40p
10p CHEAPER THAN THE DAILY MAIL
AND TEN TIMES BETTER

Victory for the Gurkhas thanks to the Daily Express
FULL STORY - PAGES 10&11

WIN A MINI COOPER
SEE PAGE 2
PREMIUM RATE PHONE LINE
WORTH OVER £12,000

Picture: PAUL KINGSTON

NOW CITY SPIVS TRY TO WRECK HBOS DEAL

Traders cause huge shares slump

By **Padraic Flanagan** and **Mark Reynolds**

SPIV traders were accused last night of betting millions of pounds in a gamble which puts the rescue of Britain's biggest mortgage lender at risk.

The £12.2billion takeover of Halifax Bank of Scotland was thrown into fresh doubt after its shares took a hammering in a day of high drama in the City.

Greedy speculators were gambling millions of pounds that the Lloyds TSB deal to save HBOS, owner of the Halifax, was in danger of falling apart. At one point, shares in HBOS were down by more than 20 per cent, but they recovered slightly to end 16p down at 126p.

As the global economic crisis has worsened, both banks' share prices have fallen along with the value of the Lloyds offer for HBOS. This has prompted the spivs to gamble that Lloyds may have to reprice the deal.

The spivs moved in despite growing anger at the City's excesses, where huge fortunes are being made by speculators on the back of reckless gambles with

TURN TO PAGE 5

No money worries for £7m Euro lotto winner (and she's only 18) SEE PAGE THREE

A *A front page of the* Daily Express

Web address: advertises online content

Masthead: the title block of the newspaper

Date line: date of publication

Slogan: reinforces the identity of the paper

Kicker: an article designed to jump out from the rest of the page

Pug: usually placed towards the corner of the paper to grab attention (price)

Headline

Strapline: a sub-heading usually printed below the headline

By-line: names the reporter who wrote the article

Leader: this is the lead story chosen for the front page

Caption: helps the reader interpret the images

Standfirst: the introductory paragraph, often in bold to grab the reader

Declining sales

In recent years, newspapers have faced increasing competition from other areas of the media. While circulation figures have declined, newspapers have responded in different ways. Some newspapers have become more like magazines, offering increasing numbers of supplements to entice different audiences. Others have become more celebrity- and scandal-focused. A popular strategy used by all the dailies are special offers and give-aways. These may include anything from scratch cards to DVDs.

DAILY EXPRESS

THE WORLD'S GREATEST NEWSPAPER www.express.co.uk SATURDAY SEPTEMBER 27, 2008 70p

FREE HEALTHY ALPRO SOYA CREAM FOR EVERY READER AT TESCO Sainsbury's WAITROSE

PLUS JUST CUT OUT THE VOUCHER ON PAGE 47 AND GET YOURS TODAY

PLUS FREE DANCE CLASSES FOR EVERY READER WITH OUR 2-FOR-1 OFFER

CALL OR GO ON-LINE TO BOOK SEE PAGE 47

GET £1 OFF OK!, hot AND OK! USA – 3 GREAT MAGAZINES PAGE 39 CUT OUT VOUCHER

SALES BONANZA AND SUNSHINE

For goodness sake let's all cheer up

By Martyn Brown and Louise Barnett

AT last, news to put a smile on our faces – the country is in for a double dose of sun and shopping cheer this weekend.

In a much-needed break from economic doom and gloom, temperatures are set to soar to 70F.

To add to the warm glow after the miserable summer, shoppers can look forward to a glittering array of cut-price offers. Even petrol is set to cost 2p a litre less than a week ago. In fact, the only problem for many over the next two days will be whether to head to the beach or the high street.

Most of Britain is expected to bask in sunshine today, enjoying temperatures warmer than parts of the Mediterranean.

If you don't want to lose out on the Indian summer but are worried about missing out on a bargain at the shops, fear not – the weather will be just as good

TURN TO PAGE 8

TORN APART: Alan Farthing and murder victim Jill Dando

Dando's fiancé becomes Queen's doctor

SEE PAGE 5

B *A front page that uses enticements to tackle declining sales*

Activity

1 Look at the front page of the *Daily Express* in **B**.

a Identify the different methods used to entice readers to buy the paper.

b Who are the enticements on the *Daily Express* aimed at? What does this tell you about the readership of the paper?

c What other enticements and give-aways do newspapers offer their readers?

4.4 The language of newspapers

What makes a newspaper?

Individual newspapers may vary in style but all of them share certain common conventions. Articles are written in columns; they use headlines, sub-headings and quotations. Photographs are used, accompanied by a caption.

The headline

The most prominent feature of any article is the headline. Recent research showed that on average eight out of 10 people read the headline, but only two out of 10 went on to read the rest of the article. Front page headlines are particularly important as they aim to grab the audience's attention and help sell the newspaper. Headlines are usually short and catchy. The tabloids place particular value on headlines, which often dominate the front page.

A *Some conventions of headlines*

Playing with a well-known phrase	How do you solve a problem like Korea? – *Sun*
Emotive language	Gotcha! – *Sun*
A pun	Sad-dammed – *Daily Mirror*
Nicknames and abbreviations	Posh and Becks in baby bid – *Sun*
Alliteration	Paddy Pantsdown – *Sun*

The copy

The articles that appear in newspapers are written by reporters and called the **copy**. News stories are generally written in a certain style and order.

1 Often readers do not read the whole article, so reporters try to include the basic facts of the story in the first paragraph. This should include Who? What? Where? When? and Why? This first paragraph aims to hook the reader into reading the rest of the article.
2 Next the article goes into greater detail and explanation for the news story.
3 Quotations are then included from people/groups involved in the story. Often an article will include quotes from different viewpoints, so as to provide a balanced report.
4 Finally, news stories often end with information about what may happen next.

Objectives

To learn about the language and conventions of newspapers.

"I always said those implants were dangerous".

B *Tabloid headlines often play on words*

Activity

1 Using current news stories, create five catchy tabloid headlines.

Key terms

Copy: a printed article in a newspaper.

Photojournalist: a journalist who uses photographs to tell a story.

Paparazzi: photographers who specialise in taking candid pictures of celebrities.

The photograph

As with the headline, a good photograph is vital for grabbing the attention of the audience. Newspaper photographs can be very powerful, and sometimes tell the story in their own right. Some photographs are very famous and have become the defining images of certain historical events.

Newspapers use different kinds of photographs. Quality newspapers sometimes employ **photojournalists**. These are photographers who specialise in news photography. Their photographs aim to tell a story and give a fair and accurate representation of events. Popular tabloids sometimes use the **paparazzi**. The paparazzi are well paid for their images and, following tip-offs, will spend hours waiting to snatch a picture of a famous person.

C *Paparazzi*

Captions

Photographs are often accompanied by captions. Captions anchor an image and help the reader interpret the photograph. The language of a caption rarely just describes the image; instead it adds to the angle of the accompanying article.

D

E

Activities

2 For the photographs shown in **D** and **E**, write a caption for each that gives the image a negative interpretation.

3 For each photograph, write a caption that gives the image a positive interpretation.

4 Choose one of your captions. Write a headline to go with the image and your chosen caption.

Extension activity

In recent years the paparazzi have been criticised for infringing famous people's privacy. Do you think people in the public eye should be protected from the paparazzi? Give reasons for your answer.

4.5 Selecting the news

News values

The most important person working for a newspaper is the editor. It is his or her job to decide which stories the newspaper will cover, in what depth, and which stories to feature on the front page. You will notice that different newspapers often choose to report different news stories, and this is because editors will select stories that they think will appeal to their target audience and stories that fit in with the values of the newspaper. The criteria editors use for selecting news stories are called **news values**.

Galtung and Ruge

In 1965, media researchers Galtung and Ruge examined different news stories. They discovered that editors tended to select certain types of news story. From their findings, they produced the following list of news values. Editors will look for news stories that contain a number of these factors:

- **Negativity:** bad news is generally more news-worthy than positive stories, e.g. tragedies, death, disasters, murder.
- **Closeness to home:** readers are more interested in stories that are closer to them geographically.
- **Recency:** newspapers focus on recent events.
- **Size:** big stories generate more interest than small ones.
- **Simplicity:** what is the meaning of an event? Readers are attracted to stories that are straightforward and clear.
- **Meaningfulness:** how meaningful is the story to the audience? British newspapers are more likely to report an international news story if British people are involved.
- **Unexpected:** stories that are different or unusual are newsworthy.
- **Currency:** some stories continue to be newsworthy because they stay in the public eye and remain current.
- **Elite nations:** the media pays more attention to powerful nations and organisations.
- **Elite people:** famous and 'important' people are newsworthy.
- **Personalisation:** stories that focus on a particular person are often newsworthy. While people relate to human interest stories, an entire industry has grown up around reporting about the lives of celebrities.
- **Continuity:** as a story unfolds it may have a continuing impact over a period of time, e.g. a war.
- **Exclusivity:** if a newspaper is the first to **break** a story, it can make it highly newsworthy. Newspapers frequently highlight the word 'exclusive' to draw attention to this type of story.
- **Predictability:** does the story match the media's and audience's expectations? Newspapers are more likely to report on stories that confirm their preconceived ideas.

Objectives

To learn about how news stories are chosen.

"People everywhere confuse what they read in newspapers with the news."

A J Liebling, US journalist

Brilliant! So where was the actress when she fell over?
Daily Tabloid

A *Newspaper editors are always looking for a scoop*

Activities

1. Why do you think bad news is reported more than good news?
2. Why do you think audiences are interested in stories about celebrities?
3. Why are unexpected stories newsworthy?
4. Read the quotation at the top of the page. What do you think it means?

POPE CONDEMNS RELIGIOUS VIOLENCE IN INDIA

ROBO-SKELETON LETS PARALYSED GIRL WALK

COMPUTER VIRUS ON INTERNATIONAL SPACE STATION

INJURY SCARE FOR ENGLAND FOOTBALL ACE

MP IN DRUGS SCANDAL

HEARTBREAK IN THE *BIG BROTHER* HOUSE

GB POPULATION TO SWELL TO 76 MILLION

EARTHQUAKE IN CHINA

BREAKFAST FRY-UP LINKED TO CANCER

THE GOVERNMENT PREDICTS ECONOMIC SLOWDOWN

Activities

Read the headlines on this page:

5 For each headline, identify its news value.

6 Which headlines might feature in a popular tabloid?

7 Which headlines might feature in a quality newspaper?

8 Why do you think the quality and popular press focus on different news values?

Extension Activity

1 Examine two daily newspapers from the same day.

- **a** Make a list of the main news stories in both papers.
- **b** Identify the news values of the different stories.
- **c** Do the news values of the two papers differ? Explain why.

4.6 Controlled assessment: Assignment 1

Introduction

Having studied newspaper front pages, you need to begin planning your work for Assignment 1 of the controlled assessment. As part of AQA GCSE media studies you are required to analyse the front pages of *two* popular newspapers, and to discuss how they appeal to their target audience. Your response needs to be approximately 400 words.

Objectives

To plan and produce your analysis of two popular newspaper front pages.

Analysing newspaper front pages

Step 1

- What is the name and type of each newspaper you have chosen to analyse?
- Who is the target audience for the newspapers?

Step 2

- Using the correct terminology, describe the layout and style of each front page.
- How has colour been used?
- What is the overall impact of the layout, colour and style? How would it appeal to the target audience?

Remember

You must analyse the front pages of two popular newspapers.

Step 3

- Look at the photographs. How have they been used on the front pages?
- What is the impact of the images on the target audience?
- How have captions been used to anchor the image?

Step 4

- Examine the mastheads. What are the connotations of the masthead?
- If there is a logo, what does this tell you about the identity of the newspaper?
- How is language used in the headlines and text? How would it appeal to the target audience?
- What type of news stories are featured on the front pages? How would they attract the target audience?
- Describe any offers or enticements on the front pages. How do these appeal to the target audience?

Step 5

- Conclude with a summary of each newspapers front page design and its appeal to the target audience.

links

You might like to refer back to pages 64–65 and 66–67 on the layout and style of newspaper front pages.

What one student did

A is an extract of a media studies student's written analysis of how the *Sun* newspaper appeals to its audience. Notice that the student uses media language in her analysis (terms such as 'splash' 'headline' and 'intertextuality'). The handwritten comments in red are from the teacher, who also uses underlining to show where the analysis is making good points. Remember, this is just an extract. You have approximately 400 words in which to complete your analysis.

AQA Examiner's tip

When analysing a media text, you need to go beyond describing what you see; you need to explain *why* it has been designed/written a certain way.

Analysis of how The Sun Newspaper appeals to it's audience.

The Sun is the most popular and the biggest selling British newspaper, selling around 9 million copies a day. It is considered to be the 'typical' British newspaper, and with it only costing 35 pence, it is massively popular amongst British people.

Using Blumler and Katz Uses and Gratification theory, we can state that The Sun satisfies it's readers by informing, educating and entertaining them. It also states that The Sun offers an escapism element to it and allows the readers to identify with the real-life situations featured in their newspaper. Another aspect of Blumler and Katz is that newspapers create social interaction. *Aud Theory*

The front page of The Sun is very informative, including some of the top stories featured in the magazine that are most likely to draw people's attention. The splash headline of this particular issue of the Sun is 'Hey Hey we're the Junkies' which is written in big, bold writing. This is so that the potential readers are able to see the text from a distance. *ML* The text gradually gets smaller so that it draws the readers in to read the rest of the story. They use bold font colours such as black and red. The connotations of the colour black are darkness, seriousness, and a generally negative impact to it. This can represent some of the more serious, crime-related stories that The Sun covers, such as this particular story about some drug addicts going cold turkey in prison. The connotations of the colour red are love, romance and lust. This indicates the amount of sex-related stories that are covered in The Sun. Their readers tend to be less educated than readers of a broadsheet newspaper, like The Times for instance. The Sun is aimed at the strata C2-E which are generally unemployed people, or people of a low educational achievement. This is why the language needs to be informative but in a simple way, possibly with a bit of humour. *Aud*

The front page of The Sun is also considered to be entertaining to its readers. The Sun uses various techniques to make it entertaining, including humorous splash headlines and nudity. There is nearly always a photo of a female with little clothing on. This is done to attract its male readers. There is a photo of Myleene Klass wearing a bikini on the front page. Myleene fits into the stereotype of female beauty, according to The Sun. *Rep* She is aged between 17-25, slim and pretty. There is an example of intertextuality because the picture was from the TV programme I'm a Celebrity...Get Me out of Here! *ML* This is a popular show with a young C2-E audience, just like the readers of the Sun. The show is very entertaining and popular, therefore the Sun wanted to share some of the enormous popularity to entertain its readers.

A *A student's work for GCSE: a written analysis of the* Sun

4.7 Controlled assessment pre-production task

Introduction

As part of AQA GCSE media studies, students are required to:

...present a pre-production task. They will need to explain their intentions, with particular reference to their use of media language and how it will appeal to the target audience.

For your controlled assessment on newspapers, you will need to design the front page of a newspaper aimed at a specific audience.

The following activity is suitable for small-group work.

Step 1 Planning

- Decide on the context and audience for your newspaper. Is it going to be a new national daily paper, a local newspaper, a community newspaper, a tabloid or broadsheet?
- Who are your potential audience?
- How are you going to design a front page that will attract your audience?
- Record your decisions on a planning sheet.

Step 2 Design

- Decide on a title for your newspaper.
- Design a masthead and logo.

Step 3 Content

- What sort of news stories are you going to cover on your front page?
- What types of images are you going to include?
- How are you going to use colour on the front page?

Step 4 Layout

- Produce a mock-up of your front page. Use frames, columns and boxes to indicate where different features will be placed.
- Decide which features to include.

Step 5 Production (Optional)

- If you choose to produce a final version of your front page, include original text and photography where possible.

Step 6 Write up

- Explain how the layout and design of your front page will attract your target audience.

Objectives

To learn how to approach the pre-production task.

Remember

The aim of a front page is to grab the audience's attention. Your front page needs to have impact.

What one student did

THE STORY

FRIDAY 8TH APRIL 2008
WWW.THESTORY.CO.UK
86P

FANCY GETTING YOUR HANDS ON THIS!?
Find out more on page 54

SHAN'S GUILT
Football star axed from FA Cup Final after drugs test. Read more page 6.

WEATHER BOMB HITS UK

UK SEES WORST WEATHER IN 18 YEARS!

EXCLUSIVE
Yesterdays storm saw Brittain's homes being destroyed by gale winds.
Several homes have been affected all over the UK, mainly in the North. People came home from work to find their fences had fallen down and in some cases even electricity poles fallen in streets.
See page 4 & 5 for more.

A *GCSE student work: a newspaper front cover*

Summary

In this chapter you have learned about:

- the diversity and impact of UK newspapers
- the differences between the popular and quality press
- the layout of front pages
- the conventions of national daily newspapers
- news values
- how to approach the controlled assessment by analysing an existing newspaper front page and then presenting ideas of your own.

5 Web-based media

Objectives

To learn about what is required to successfully complete the analysis of web-based media.

About this topic

What you will need to do

If you or your teacher chooses web-based media for Assignment 1, you will be required to analyse the home pages of *two* popular entertainment websites. There are many websites of this type available online. A good starting point could be the website *www.ew.com*, which has details and links to lots of entertainment websites. Typically, an entertainment website exists to entertain its audience. The topics that entertainment websites cover can be very broad, but all will be trying to engage their audiences using the multi-media qualities that the web has to offer.

Consider audience appeal

You will need to write about how your chosen home pages are constructed to appeal to their audiences. To do this successfully you will need to learn the appropriate media language and use it in your analysis of your chosen home pages. You could begin by giving a brief description of the various **elements** that make up the pages, but you have a limit of about 400 words, so don't go into too much detail at the level of **denotation**. Instead, concentrate on how meaning is created for an audience – the **connotations** that are suggested. You should ask yourself lots of questions about why the content of the home page you are analysing is presented in the way that it is.

Analyse the codes and conventions

The task will require you to analyse the various **codes and conventions** that are used in the construction of your chosen home pages. You will need to look carefully for ways in which the audience can interact with the pages, how the construction of the home pages appeals to the audience and how the interest of that audience is maintained.

It may be useful to compare some of the elements in each of the home pages and discuss any differences or similarities you find.

A breakdown of the tasks

In a nutshell, you need to complete the following tasks when carrying out your analysis of the home pages selected:

- Discuss the various conventions used in each home page.
- Use appropriate media language in your discussion.
- Say something about representation and institutions.
- Discuss how the various elements work to engage the interest of an audience.

Key terms

Elements: the individual parts that together make up a web page.

Denotation: what we can see in a media text.

Connotation: the message that a media text might give or suggest.

Codes and Conventions: the typical features that we would expect from a particular text, the 'rules'.

Following your analysis, you will need to use what you have learned to design your own home page for an entertainment website. Take into consideration the target audience for the website – their age, gender and interests is a good place to start. How will you cater for this audience in your website? Using your knowledge of web-based media, you will write a brief report (no more than 100 words) on your ideas.

Starter activity

Go online and find the home pages of two different entertainment websites. Give a brief description of both at the level of denotation. What similarities and what differences do you notice in each page?

Extension activity

What do you consider to be the most important elements of the home pages you have researched and why?

A *The home page of* Heat *magazine online*

B *Another entertainment website,* tv.com

AQA Examiner's tip

Ensure that your response is rich in media language. After all, this is what separates you from someone who has not had a media studies education!

5.1 Conventions of websites

The purpose of websites

Some websites provide information and others are for entertainment. Many websites blur this distinction by presenting information in an entertaining and engaging way. News websites, in particular, present news stories in a way that attempts to engage the audience. This is achieved through the interactive and multi-media qualities of the web.

Other websites offer a service or encourage us to buy certain products. And then there are personal websites. You may have your own **blog** or a personal home page on MySpace, Bebo or Facebook. These social networking websites have become very popular and further diminish the distinction between the audience and the producer.

Objectives

- To learn a range of media terminology relevant to the analysis of website home pages.
- To identify the conventions on various web pages.

Key terms

Blog: a website where entries are made in journal style. Blogs can be found on all different topics. Sometimes they are called 'web logs'.

Home page: the first page of a website that the user will come across. This page usually contains links to other pages on the website.

Activity

1 Select the home pages of three different websites. What is the purpose of each website? Who do you think would visit these websites? Try to think of the audience's age, gender and interests.

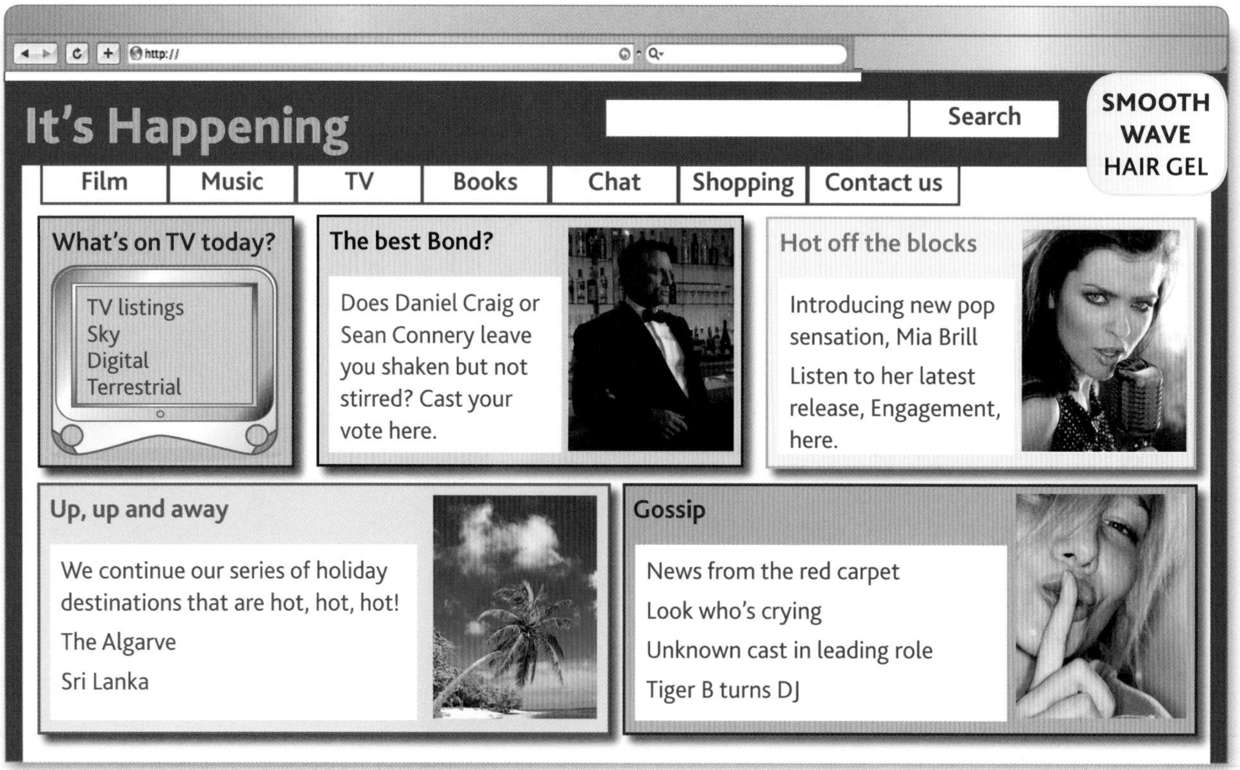

A *The conventions of a website home page*

A website's **home page** is usually the most important page, containing various elements that provide information in their own right or offer the audience the opportunity to interact with the page, navigating to other parts of the page or the website.

Although the content varies on different home pages, there are many similar conventions which are used. In particular, the layout of many websites follows a similar pattern. Any variations are dependent upon the purpose of the website, the genre and the needs of the target audience.

Websites will contain a number of these factors:

- **Headings:** used throughout some web pages to split the content into manageable sections. There may also be sub-headings, which can further direct the user to a particular piece of information.
- **Copy:** the main body of text, often presented in boxes.
- **Hyperlinks:** these can be either words or images that when clicked upon will take you to another page of the website.
- **Scrolling text:** areas of text which the user can scroll through. Scrolling text is useful because it allows a large amount of text to be placed within a relatively small box.
- **Images:** used in almost every website – sometimes used as a link to another part of the website.
- **Video:** thanks to broadband, many websites can safely go beyond featuring text and static images to incorporate video.
- **Sound:** used on many websites. You may hear a sound as the cursor rolls over some part of a website. Music is often used in websites as an introduction on the home page. This can set up certain expectations for the viewer and establish the tone of the rest of the website.
- **Drop-down menus:** these usually have an arrow at the end of a rectangle box. When you click on the arrow, a menu drops down. The user can then make a choice of where to go next.
- **Search box:** usually a box in which the user can type a word or words relating to the content they are trying to locate.
- **Banners:** usually found across the top of a website's home page. In vertical format, they are known as 'skyscrapers'. These usually contain adverts for products or services.
- **Navigation:** a series of buttons, images or text with which user can interact and find their way around a website.
- **Thumbnails:** images are sometimes displayed in reduced size. However, a full-size image can usually be accessed by clicking on the thumbnail.
- **Frames:** the content of a website is usually broken down into frames. This makes the content more manageable and easier to read.

Activity

2 Go online and find two entertainment websites. If you can, it would help to print out the home page. Try to identify some of the typical conventions already discussed by annotating the page.

Extension activity

Conduct a class survey to find out why people use the web and what websites they visit. If possible, do the same activity with an older audience and compare the results.

AQA Examiner's tip

Focus on learning how these conventions are used to engage the interest of an audience keen on entertainment websites.

Did you know ??????

British computer scientist Sir Tim Berners-Lee (1955–) invented the World Wide Web (www) in the late 1980s, to help scientists share their research. People soon started using it to share all kinds of information.

Every website has a unique address which is typed into the address bar, usually found at the top of the browser bar. This address is referred to as a URL – Uniform Resource Locater.

links

Go to **www.technorati.com** and click on 'blogs' to find examples of literally hundreds of blogs on a range of subjects.

5.2 Analysis of home pages

Now that you have learned some of the media terminology used to analyse web pages, we will apply this knowledge in the analysis of two entertainment website home pages: BBC Radio 1 and Spire FM.

Objectives

To learn how to analyse entertainment websites using appropriate media terminology.

The home pages

The home page is the first page that a user will come across when typing in a web address. The home page for BBC Radio 1 can be found at www.bbc.co.uk/radio1. The content will be different from **A**, but the layout and design of the web page will be the same. The home page for Spire FM can be found at www.spirefm.co.uk. Once again the content may be different from what you see in **B**, but the layout and design will be similar.

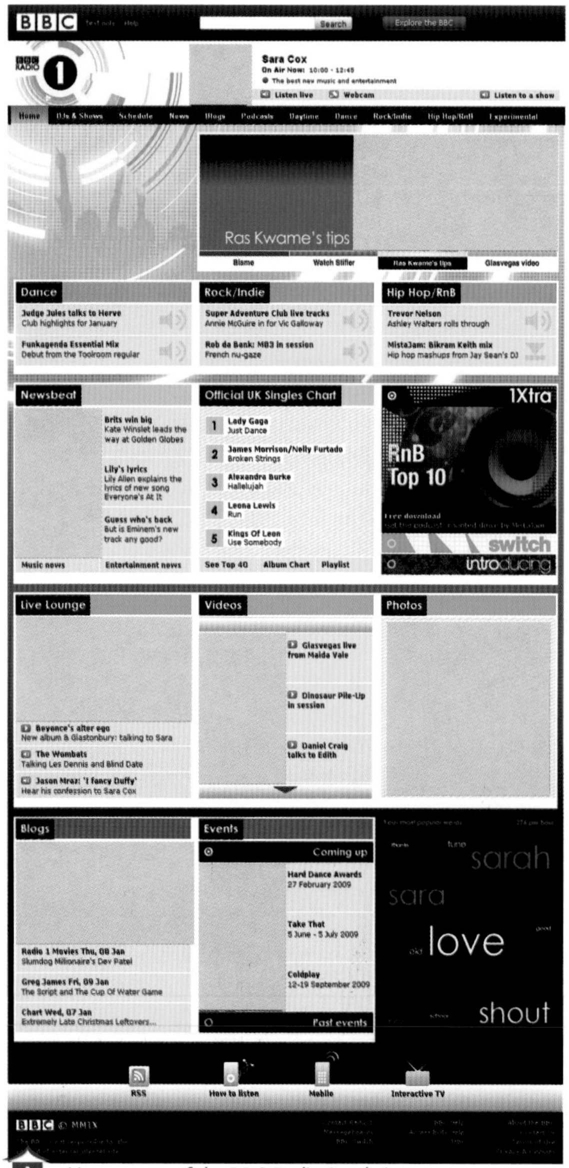

A *Home page of the BBC Radio 1 website*

B *Home page of the Spire FM website*

The home page for Radio 1's website is full of promise! The audience can be taken to various places in the website and have various experiences. This is achievable through clicking on the different links.

- We can listen 'Live' to the programme playing at any given time.
- We can visit the Live Lounge.
- We can view live via a webcam the studio from which programmes are broadcast.
- We can find out information about the DJs.
- We can see information about the UK chart singles.
- We can get up-to-date entertainment news.

All of the above can be accessed through the various links on the home page.

Layout and design

Consistency in design and **layout** in any website is important. In the case of the BBC, this helps to build an awareness of the brand with the audience. The colours, text, logo and general design become familiar and easily recognisable to the audience.

How we look at web pages

Web pages are not just thrown together. The placing of each element is carefully considered by web designers to give maximum impact and to make a web page user-friendly. Over the years a set of conventions has developed that underpins website design. This has, in part, been influenced by repetition of design, but also in part by research that suggests particular patterns in the way we view a website.

The pattern that our eyes follow as we scan a web page is shown in **C**.

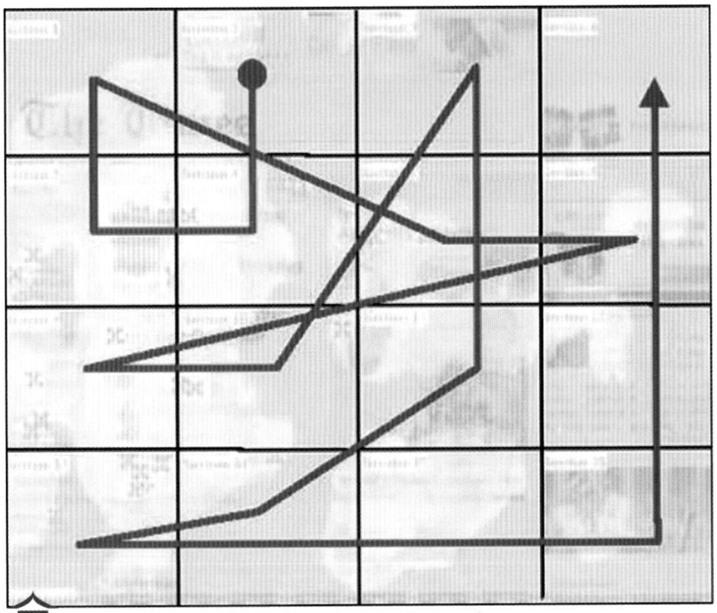

C *An average overall viewing sequence for a web page*

Eyetrack III studied the viewing patterns of people as they looked at online content. We could use this pattern as a starting point to analyse how viewers read a web page.

Activities

1. Go online to the Spire FM website. What does the home page promise the audience?
2. Go online to the BBC's home page: www.bbc.co.uk. Navigate your way around the website. Is the design and layout consistent across the website? What colours, style of text and other design elements are used to maintain this consistency?
3. Study the home page of BBC Radio 1. Where do you look first, second, third and so on? Try this with other website home pages. Does your pattern of looking follow that shown in **C**?

Key terms

Layout: the way that the different elements of a web page are set out.

Did you know ??????

According to a recent survey by Netcraft, in January 2009 there were 185,497,213 websites available for viewing online.

Extension activity

Undertake further testing of Eyetrack III's theory. Print out the home pages of several websites and use them as a basis for your research. Ask friends and family members to circle the part of the page that their eye is drawn to first on viewing the page. Write up the results.

kerboodle!

The positioning of elements that make up a web page

According to the viewing pattern in **C**, the first place that the audience will look when viewing a website is near the top left-hand corner. This is where the BBC's logo is to be found on the home page of the Radio 1 website. This serves to anchor the meaning of the website and reassures the viewer that the website reflects the quality one would expect from the BBC. The logo on the Spire FM website is in a similar position.

Moving on, the next area of a web page that our eyes come into contact with, according to the research, is the link buttons. These are the main elements of interaction to other pages.

Activity

Study the home page for the commercial radio station in your area. How is a sense of community maintained through the various elements? How is the user invited to interact with the page?

Links

There are many links to be found on both of the home pages for these radio stations. These provide a level of interactivity for the audience and are the key convention that separates interactive media from print. On the Spire FM website there are links to take the user to various other pages which provide the local community with information on local events. There are opportunities for the user to interact with the radio station through email, text and phone. Users can also be part of the spirefmfacebook, with the promise that they may see someone they already know! The sense of a local community is strong. National events are also recognised – users are asked to respond to a survey on a newsworthy topic.

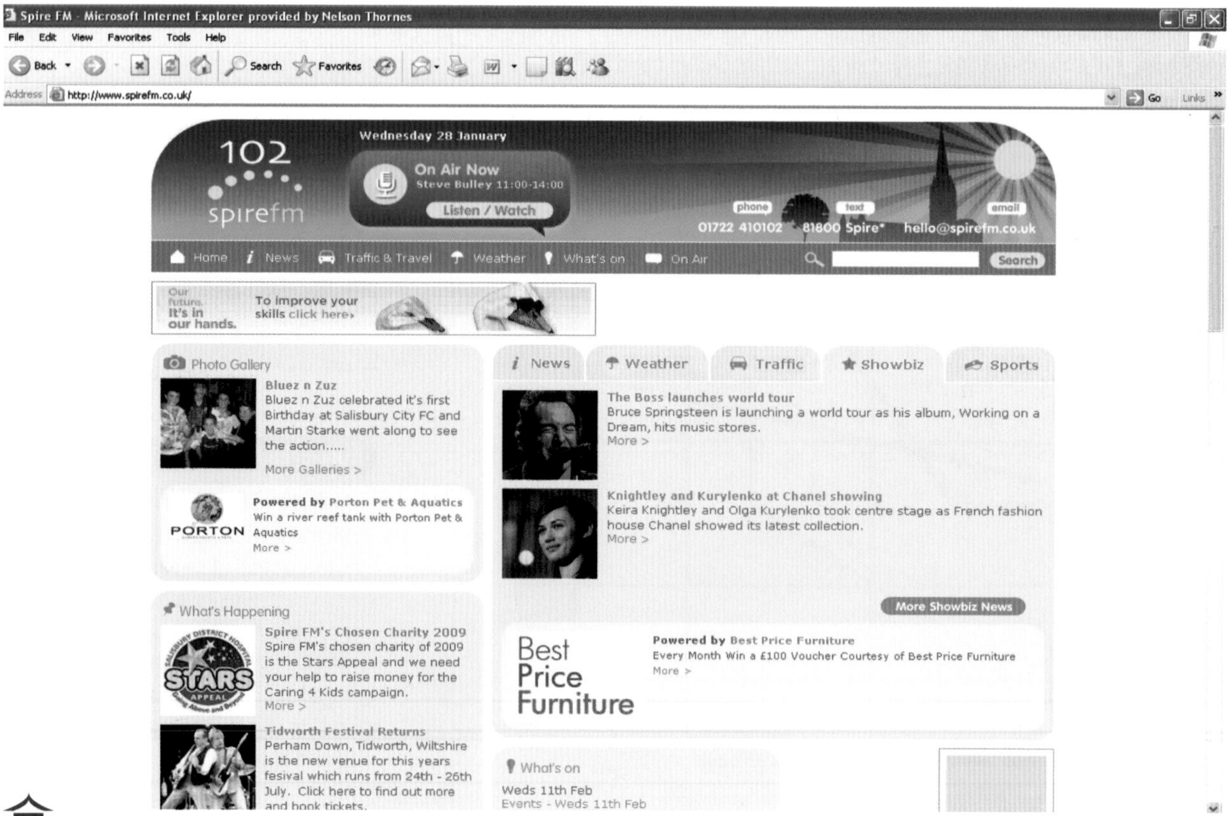

D *A close-up of Spire FM's links on the home page*

Current information

An important aspect of both the Radio 1 and Spire FM home pages is that they are up-to-date. There are several signs on each site to suggest that this is the case. The Spire FM website has the date at the top and information on local traffic and travel problems. The user is informed of who is 'On Air Now' and is asked to listen live to their show. The Radio 1 website invites the user to view the studio via the webcam. This not only serves to give a sense of immediacy but also gives a sense of being part of the event.

Images

The images are used to attract the audience and in some cases to give a visual reference to the names of the DJs. Each photograph on both home pages is accompanied by text. The text serves to anchor the meaning of the images and to set up certain expectations as to what lies beyond it. Without the text, the image is ambiguous and so could have many connotations.

Sound

Sound is an obvious important element on radio station websites. As well as the usual clicks when the user rolls over a link, there is the opportunity to listen to the stations' output online.

E *Many radio stations have a webcam which allows you to view DJs at work*

Mode of address

The various elements combined give a certain **mode of address** or 'feel' to the audience. An audience can recognise themselves and their interests through the content and the way that this content is presented – the colours, style and tone of the text as well as the images used all contribute to the mode of address. The mode of address for the Spire FM website is a friendly, informal one and one that often speaks directly to the user. On the Spire FM website, the audience is invited to 'Upload your images' – a direct form of address.

AQA *Examiner's tip*

All website home pages are constructed to appeal to a specific audience. This is done through the presentation of certain content. However, your analysis should not simply discuss what is presented but how it is presented.

Search box

Each home page contains a search box which enables the users to interact with the page and search for information across each site.

Advertisements

Advertising forms an important aspect of the home page for Spire FM but is clearly lacking from the BBC home page. This reflects their respective commercial and public service interests.

Did you know ??????

In 2007/08, the BBC spent £129 million on its online content.

kerboodle!

5.3 The role of the audience

In the previous pages we looked at how to analyse website home pages. We will now look closer at the role of the audience in interpreting information online.

Objectives

To learn about the role of the audience in the consumption of online material.

Different websites – different audiences

All media products are aimed at specific audiences, and websites are no different. The audience for a particular website is reflected in the content of that website.

Audiences can be categorised using different methods. One of the main methods is by **demographics**. This involves describing audiences by their age, gender, interests, social class and by where they live.

The audience for Spire FM is different from that for Radio 1. This is partly defined by demographics. Spire FM serves the needs of those living in south Wiltshire, while Radio 1's audience is drawn nationwide. The websites, however, extend the geographical location of the audience internationally. Anyone can listen to the stations' output in most regions of the world. Kerry Jones, the station manager at Spire FM, states that there are a large number of expats who access the radio station via the website.

Passive audience

Many claims have been made about the media's influence on audiences throughout history. Many position the audience as passive receptors of media information who are easily influenced by media content.

The hypodermic needle effect

This theory suggests that the media can influence a very large number of people directly by 'injecting' them with messages, which result in a particular audience response. The flow of information is direct from the sender to the receiver – the passive audience is directly influenced by the message.

The Nazi propaganda in Germany is often cited as a prime example of the powerful influence of the media and, in the 1950s, advertising was seen as something that could persuade people to buy products in ways they did not realise.

The active audience

Many, however, have doubted the ease with which the media can influence an audience. Rather than seen as being passive recipients of media messages, audiences are seen as active participants in constructing and interpreting their own meanings.

This position changed the notion of 'what the media do to audiences' to 'what do audiences do with the media?'

Activities

1. Go to **www.bbc.co.uk/commissioning** to find details of how the BBC pictures the audience for Radio 1. How is this reflected in the home page for Radio 1?
2. Choose an entertainment website and draw up a list of reasons why an audience might use that website.

Extension activity

Imagine you have been commissioned to create the home page for an entertainment website of your choice. Try to describe the audience that you want to target.

links

Go to **www.mediauk.com**, click on 'radio' and then on the letter 's' to obtain detailed data about the audience for Spire FM.

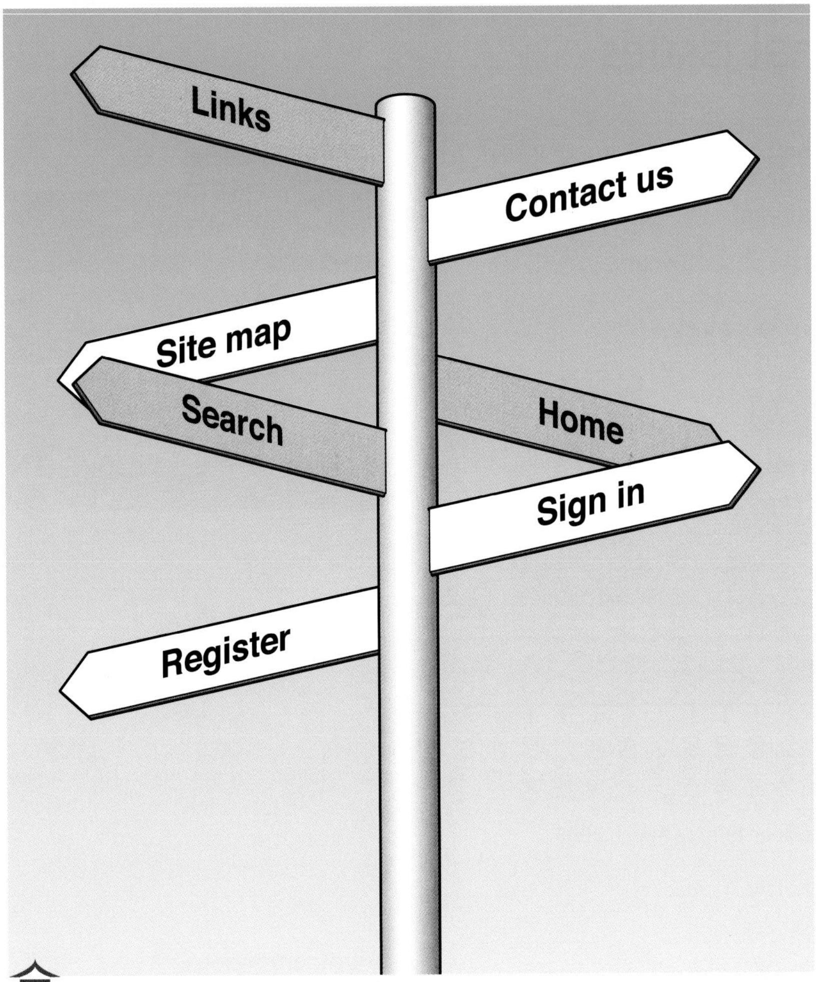

A

Did you know ??????

On 30 October 1938 (the eve of Halloween) a theatre group in America broadcast its edition of HG Wells's *War of the Worlds*. Radio programming was interrupted with a news bulletin stating that Martians had begun an invasion of Earth. About 1 million people in America believed what they heard and mass hysteria followed!

Remember

Audiences enjoy interacting with web pages, but too many choices may leave them with a fragmented experience.

So what has this to do with audiences and websites?

Well, the notion of the active audience is crucial to an understanding of how audiences interact with web pages.

The home page of any entertainment website invites the audience to actively interact with the content. On the home page for the Radio 1 website, for instance, audiences have the opportunity to customise their own page. They can download various items and have a user experience based on their individual interests. They can navigate around the website and in so doing construct their own narratives. Far from being passive recipients of the information, the audience is actively encouraged to interact.

AQA Examiner's tip

Have a clear idea of the audience for the website home pages you are analysing. This will help you assess how their needs and interests are served by the layout and content of each website.

links

For further discussion on how audiences use the media, see the reference to uses and gratifications on pages 12–13.

5.4 Institutional issues

The growth of the web has been phenomenal. In 1993, there was a total of 130 websites and according to the latest statistics (4 April 2008) there are now more than 162 million.

The chart in **A** shows this growth over the last 18 years.

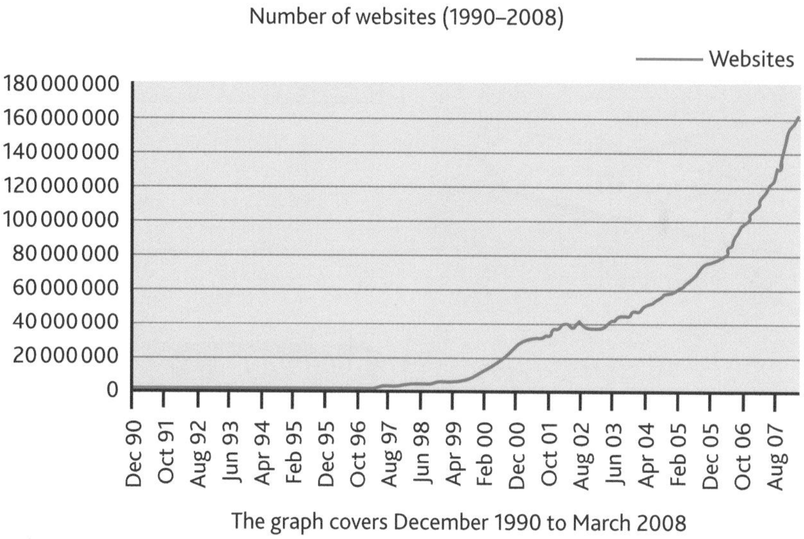

A *How we got from 1 to 162 million websites on the internet*

Objectives

To learn the difference between commercial and non-commercial radio station websites and how these are funded.

To learn about some of the issues surrounding the regulation of the World Wide Web.

This growth has partly been possible because of a growth in technology. The first websites were fairly simple with large areas of static text, few images and no video. Interactive elements were few – the main objective was to provide information.

Many organisations have seen the potential of the web as a means of extending their activities. Table **B** shows the number of visitors to the BBC's website in March 2007. The total for the month was 90 076 709.

Did you know ??????

A recent survey by blog tracking firm Technorati suggested that every day 100 000 new blogs are created and 1.3 million items are posted.

Activities

1. Compare the first Apple website, at http://macenstein.com/default/archives/1087, with the one today, at www.apple.com. How has the user experience changed?

2. Go online and research how the figures in table **B** compare with the figures in 2000. How do you account for the increase or decrease in visitors? Why do you think this information is important to the BBC?

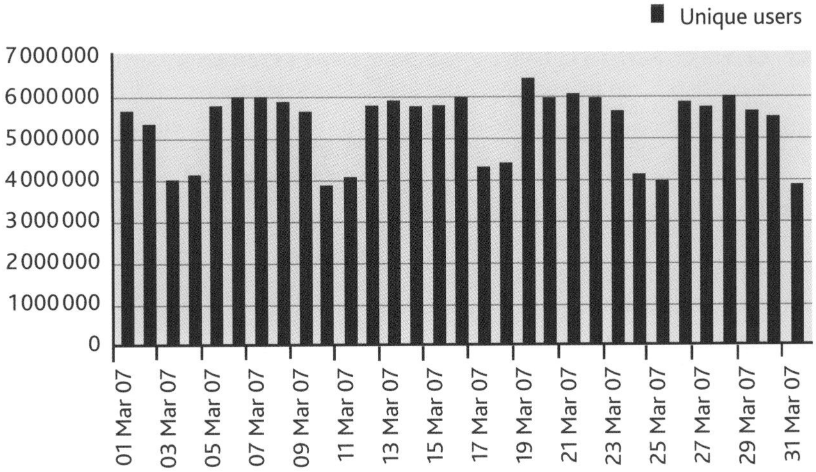

B *The number of users of the BBC website*

Funding the BBC's website

The BBC is funded through the licence fee. The revenue raised from this fee is used to pay for the services provided by the BBC, including its online content. The BBC is known as a public service broadcaster (PSB) and is free from commercial constraints. This is why you will not find any advertising on its website, other than advertisements that promote the BBC's own products.

Funding Spire FM's website

Spire FM is a commercial radio station. This means that it receives the major part of its funding through selling advertising on air and on the website. The website is produced and updated in-house, so the cost to the company of running the website is minimal. The cost of advertising on the website varies but typically a micro-site advert will cost in the region of £400 per calendar month (in 2008). The income generated from this form of advertising constitutes 3 per cent of the total income of the station. This helps to support the various activities of the station.

Regulation

All the content that is to be found on websites is subject to the general law of the land, in the same way as any other offline activity. However, this is not a heavily regulated activity. **Internet Service Providers** do have the power to take down inappropriate content when they are notified of its existence but with the rising number of websites, this is a difficult task to manage. The difficulties are further compounded when you take into account that the internet is without any geographical boundaries. How do you regulate material that is uploaded in one country and downloaded in another? There are many individuals and organisations involved – where does the control begin and end?

Research activity

How much is the licence fee today and what was the total revenue raised from it in 2007? In what other ways has the BBC attempted to raise revenue to support its various activities?

Activities

3 Study the home pages of two other commercial radio stations. Roughly, what percentage of each page is taken up by advertising? Contact the radio stations and try to determine the income generated from advertising on their websites.

4 Do you think there is a need to regulate the content of websites? Whose responsibility should this be?

Key terms

Internet Service Provider (ISP): a company that collects a monthly or annual fee in exchange for providing the subscriber with internet access.

5.5 Controlled assessment: Assignment 1

Introduction

As part of AQA GCSE Media Studies, and having studied the home pages of two entertainment websites, you need to begin planning your work for Assignment 1 of the controlled assessment. You are required to produce an analysis of two entertainment website home pages and discuss how they appeal to their target audience. Your response needs to be approximately 400 words.

Objectives

To plan and produce your analysis of two popular entertainment website home pages.

Analysing popular website home pages

Step 1

- What are the names of the website home pages you have chosen and what is their URL?
- Who is the target audience for each home page? Can you construct an audience profile?
- Are these mainstream or niche audiences?

Step 2

- Study the content of the home pages in detail and describe the layout of each page.
- Try to use appropriate media terminology: headings, links, scrolling text, animation and sound, search boxes, banner advertising and so on. When images (still or moving) are used you should refer to shot type, camera angles and lighting.
- What connotations are suggested by the various elements?

Step 3

- What conventions are used to enable the audience to interact with the pages?
- What do the website home pages promise the audience?
- Are there any advertisements present? What do these tell you about the intended audience for the website?

Step 4

- Can you say anything about how the website home pages represent people and/or places? Are they positive or negative representations and are stereotypes used?
- How might the websites be funded – through advertising and/or subscription?

Step 5

- Overall, explain how the home pages are designed to appeal to their target audience.

What one student did

www.kerrang.com and www.redstorm.com

I have chosen two different entertainment websites to analyse. One website is an online entertainment site related to a real magazine that specialises in music and the other is a game company's website – Redstorm.
The first website; www.kerrang.com is a specialist music entertainment site that covers the genre of rock and heavy metal. You could call it a niche website as it is for a very particular audience. The target audience for this website can be defined by their interest in the world of rock and metal music and the lifestyles that surround it. They tend to be mostly male and are aged between 16-24. They are likely to be in the social economic class of C2's and D's. This audience enjoy receiving their entertainment through the web and love engaging with the interactive qualities that the web has to offer. So how does the website appeal to this audience? The Kerrang home page is constructed to incorporate the audiences interests and demographical statistics by providing puff pieces about various rock artists and their personal lives. The audience feel they can get closer to some of their idols and be privy to 'exclusive' information. The content of the home page is broken down by the use of headings and subheadings, directing the audience to what is important. There are several hyperlinks to additional features such as rock videos – the audience is encouraged to navigate their way around the site. Thumbnail images of various artists are used to entice the audience and act as enigmas, encouraging the audience to delve further into the site. The layout of the homepage consists of very dark and gothic colours suggesting connotations of the heavy rock genre. The background has a scratched and eerie appearance reflecting the typical conventions of rock/metal music. This makes the website easily recognisable and very appealing to its target audience. The font used on this homepage also follows the codes and conventions of rock/metal genre as the logo is bold and modern, with a distressed appearance. The audience is promised more when they sign up to the 'noiseletter' and can even access other products of the company via the homepage. The homepage has many gif. images that are constantly changing. These are anchored by the text and in effect, gives the impression that Kerrang is current, providing endless amounts of entertainment regarding the target audience's favourite topic. This engages their attention for longer, as they want to wait until they have seen all of the gif. images.

Blaise Persaud

A *Student work for GCSE: an extract from an analysis of an entertainment website*

A is an extract of a Media Studies student's written analysis of two entertainment website home pages. There is a clear grasp of media terminology associated with website analysis (headings and sub-headings, hyperlinks, thumbnails, connotations and anchorage) and an excellent attempt to define the target audience. Notice how the various elements of one home page are discussed and how the student considers the notion of appeal in relation to the target audience. This is an excellent piece of work and worthy of a high mark at GCSE though as an extract, only one home page has been considered in any depth. Remember, you are required to analyse two home pages!

AQA *Examiner's tip*

In your analysis, focus less on 'what' is presented and more on 'how' the various elements are presented and how they might be interpreted by an audience.

links

You could use one or more of the following entertainment websites for your analysis: **www.awesome-events.co.uk**, **www.ents24.com/web** and **http://fourfourtwo.com**

kerboodle!

5.6 Controlled assessment pre-production task

Introduction

As part of AQA GCSE Media Studies, students are required to:

"...present a pre-production task. They will need to explain their intentions, with particular reference to their use of media language and how it will appeal to the target audience."

For your controlled assessment on web-based media, you will need to design the home page for an entertainment website of your choice.

The following activity is suitable for small-group work.

Step 1 Planning

- Remind yourself of the genre of website you have studied and familiarise yourself with the codes and conventions associated with this genre.
- Decide on the type of entertainment home page to produce and the audience you will be targeting. It may be that your entertainment home page focuses on film, music, sport, celebrity gossip or a mixture of subjects.
- Consider how you will design the home page to attract your audience.
- Record your decisions on a design sheet.

Step 2 Design

- Decide a heading for your home page.
- Design this heading as it will appear in your home page.

Step 3 Content

- What links will you have on your home page and where will they take the user? Consider placing them within a navigation bar.
- What type of video/images will you use and how many?
- What will be the main 'copy' on your home page?
- What will be the 'mood' of your home page? What colours and style of font will you use?
- Will you use adverts on your home page?

Step 4 Layout

- Produce a draft design of your home page combining the elements from Step 3. Make sure that the layout is reflective of other home pages within the genre that you have studied.

Step 5 Production (Optional)

- If you choose to produce a final version of your home page you may wish to use an image editing program such as Photoshop.

Step 6 Write up

- Explain how the layout and design of your home page will attract your target audience.

Objectives

To learn how to approach the pre-production task.

Remember

The aim of your home page is to attract the attention of your audience and engage their interest. The home page needs to have impact!

What one student did

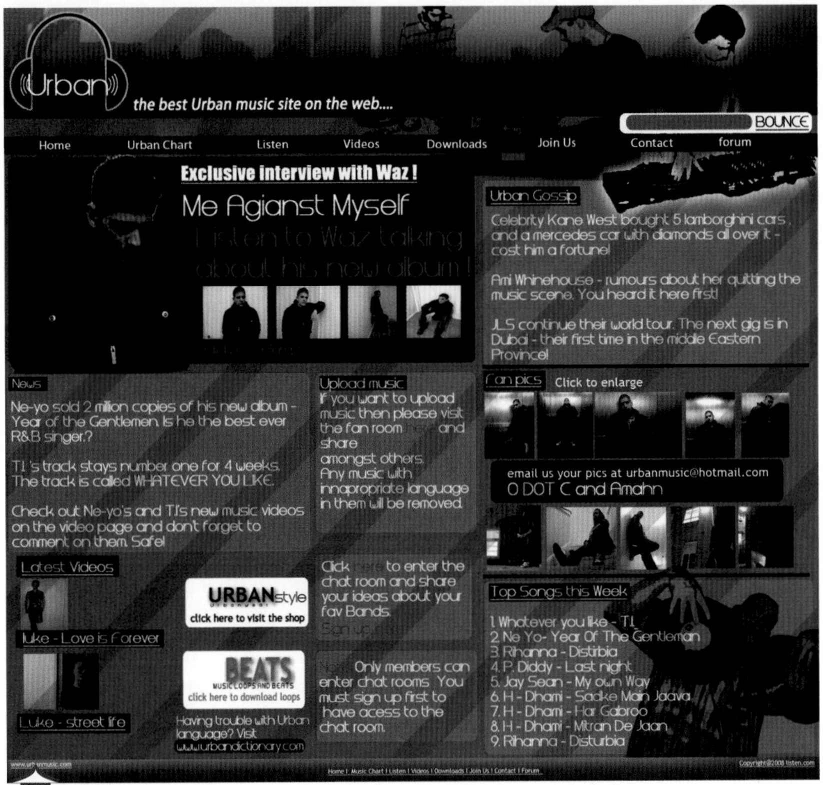

A *GCSE student work: a home page for an entertainment website*

In **A** we have the home page for a music entertainment website, created by a GCSE Media Studies student. Notice the use of original imagery as the candidate creates fictitious musicians using his family and friends. The home page contains many of the conventions we would expect to find in a website from this genre – there are headings which help split up the content, hyperlinks, navigational links, thumbnail images and a search box. The layout of the page reflects the viewing patterns described earlier, with the logo positioned in the top left-hand corner. This is a convincing piece of work that appropriately addresses the target audience. It is well worth a high grade at GCSE.

Remember

Organising the content into frames makes it easier to read and hence, a much more enjoyable user experience.

AQA Examiner's tip

The use of original imagery will greatly enhance your work and provide you with many opportunities for creative manipulation.

Summary

In this chapter, you have learned about:

- the conventions of websites
- how to analyse home pages using appropriate terminology
- the role of the audience in using website home pages
- some institutional issues surrounding websites
- how to approach the controlled assessment by analysing the home pages of two existing entertainment websites and then presenting ideas for your own.

GCSE

The controlled assessment

Assignment 2. Cross-media study

What is cross-media?

Assignment 1 focused on the topics of magazines, comics, television sitcoms, newspapers and web-based media. In studying these topics you will have analysed the codes and conventions of different media texts which have been produced for a single **media platform**. However, in the real world, the same media products often appear in a number of different **media forms** and across different media platforms. The release of a new film, for instance, will result in a media-wide campaign with material generated across different media such as television, magazines, radio, newspapers and the internet. 'Cross-media' refers to a product that appears in more than one branch of the media.

In this section of the book, which relates to Assignment 2, you will look at music promotion, advertising and marketing, and film promotion. Through each topic you will examine how these industries utilise a multi platform, cross-media approach to promoting their products.

What you will need to do

For Assignment 2, you will need to:

- Study one media topic that uses a cross-media approach.
- Focus on the key concepts of representation and institutions.
- Analyse and explain the way a media product is represented and marketed in two different media.

Your analysis and explanation should be approximately 1000 words.

Working in the same topic area, you will then:

- Present two pre-production tasks based on the promotion of a media product across two areas of the media.
- Explain how the product has been represented across the two pre-production tasks.

Objectives

To consider the meaning of 'cross-media'.

To examine an example of a media product that is promoted across different media platforms.

links

For information on representation and institutions, see pages 14–17.

An example of cross-media promotion – *The Simpsons*

The Simpsons is an American animated sitcom produced by the Fox Broadcasting Company. While the main platform for *The Simpsons* is television, it has appeared in a variety of different forms and on a variety of different media platforms.

A *Cross-media promotion of* The Simpsons

B *The teaser poster for the 2007 movie*

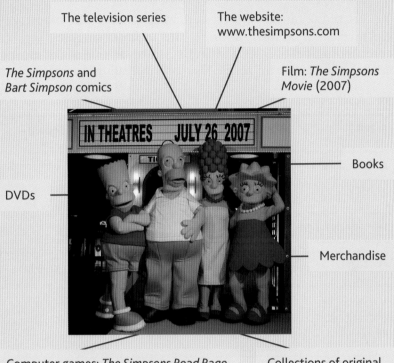

Key terms

Media platform: the technology through which we receive media products.

Media form: the distinguishing characteristics of types of media products.

Synergy: the process by which a media institution uses different products to sell another (e.g. film, video game, soundtrack).

Starter activity

- Identify the different platforms that feature *The Simpsons*.
- How do you think the use of different media has helped promote the popularity of *The Simpsons*?
- What advantages does the Fox Broadcasting Company have when promoting a product across different media?
- The promotion of *The Simpsons* through different media products is an example of synergy. Can you list other examples of synergy in the media?

Did you know ??????

Disney was one of the first media institutions to use the idea of synergy to market its animated films. In the 1930s Walt Disney granted firms the right to use Mickey Mouse on products and in advertisements.

6 Music promotion

Assignment 2

Objectives

To learn about the institutions that run the music industry.

To appreciate the different ways in which record companies promote their artists.

The music industry

Music is on the radio, it features in advertisements, it dramatises films, it is on the web. You are going to look at the music industry and examine the methods it uses to sell music to the public.

Money, money, money

The aim of the music industry is to make money. The industry sells music in a number of forms. This includes singles, merchandise, ticket sales and DVDs. However, one of the most profitable packages for music has been the album, see table **A**.

A *The best-selling albums of all time*

Artiste	Title	Year	Sales	Record label
Michael Jackson	*Thriller*	1982	108 million	Epic Records
AC/DC	*Back in Black*	1980	42 million	Atlantic Records
Whitney Houston/ various artistes	*The Bodyguard*	1992	42 million	Arista Records
The Eagles	*Their Greatest Hits (1971–5)*	1976	41 million	Asylum
The Bee Gees/ various artistes	*Saturday Night Fever*	1977	40 million	RSO
Pink Floyd	*The Dark Side of the Moon*	1973	40 million	EMI
Meat Loaf	*Bat Out of Hell*	1977	37 million	Cleveland Int.
Shania Twain	*Come on Over*	1997	36 million	Mercury
The Beatles	*Sgt. Pepper's Lonely Hearts Club Band*	1967	32 million	EMI
Led Zeppelin	*Led Zeppelin IV*	1971	32 million	Atlantic Records

Starter activity

1 In pairs, look at table **A**:

a Which of the albums or artistes have you heard of?

b What does the table tell you about the music business?

c Why do you think album sales so important to the success of an artiste?

Who are the record companies?

In table **A** you will see that each album was released on a record label. These labels are the record companies that pay for the production, promotion and distribution of the music. Every signed band or singer has signed up to a record label. Today the music industry is dominated by four large companies: Universal Music Group (25.5 per cent market share), SonyBMG (21 per cent), EMI Group (13.4 per cent) and Warner Music Group (11.3 per cent). Each company owns a number of smaller record labels and each record label has different artistes signed to it. All the record labels listed in table **A** are owned by the 'big four'. In recent years, these companies have had to make cut-backs as the internet has challenged the way the music industry has operated.

The music industry is big business. Despite recent falling CD sales, in 2008 digital music sales alone generated over $2 billion. While the big four record companies dominate the market, independent labels have over a quarter of the market share.

Research activity

Find five artistes signed to SonyBMG, Universal and EMI.

Did you know ??????

The term 'indie' originally referred to music that was independent of the major record labels. More recently the meaning has moved away from its non-mainstream origins to refer to a style of music.

Independent record labels

Independent record labels are smaller record companies that are not owned by any of the 'big four'. They are often regarded as being more in touch with the fans, and more concerned about the music than the major record companies. Unlike the majors they rarely have their own distribution channels. Examples of independent record labels include Mute and Maverick. To gain credibility, the major record companies sometimes buy up these independent record labels or launch their own nominally independent labels.

How do record companies promote their artistes?

The major record companies often spend large amounts of money promoting an artiste to generate sales.

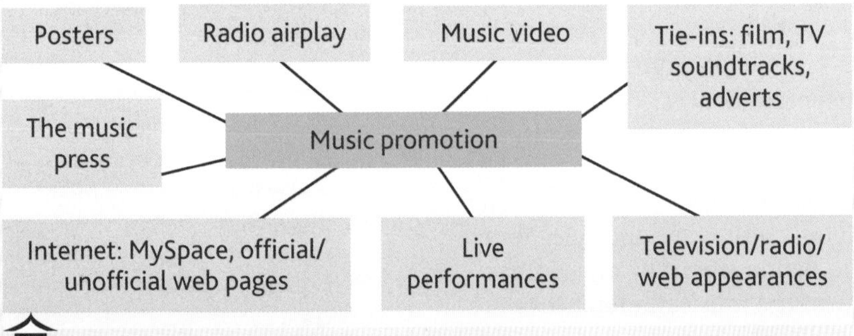

B *Ways that record companies promote music*

Starter activity

Look at the promotional methods in diagram **B**:

2 Which methods do you think are the most effective for promoting an artiste?

3 Which methods do you think are the most expensive?

4 Which methods are small independent record labels more likely to use?

6.1 Different categories of music

Which styles of music are represented by the following artistes?

A *Bob Marley*

B *Rihanna*

Objectives

To examine how the music industry categorises different styles of music.

To understand that the music industry uses these categories to target different audiences.

C *Elvis Presley*

Music tastes

Today there are hundreds of different styles of music to choose from. New styles are constantly appearing as artistes try to create different and original sounds. As a result, the popularity of these styles changes all the time. The music that you listen to now is probably quite different to the music you were listening to four years ago. It may be that your music tastes have changed as you have got older, but you will notice that some bands and singers that were popular a few years ago are no longer so successful. As tastes in music change, the music industry tries to cash in on the popularity of the latest sounds.

Audience and styles of music

Different styles of music appeal to different audiences. Try looking at your parents' CD or vinyl collection! The music industry categorises music so that it can target appropriate audiences. You will see this in record stores, radio play lists and music television. As well as listening habits, styles of music can refer to fashion, culture and lifestyle. Young people sometimes use styles of music to define who they are. Goths, Punks, Emos and Hippies are just a few of the musical references that people use.

Activities

1. In pairs, try to list as many styles of music as you can.
2. Look at your list. Which styles of music are popular today?
3. Give an example of a popular band or singer for each style that is popular today.
4. For each of these four characters, in illustration **D**, list the styles of music and the artistes they might listen to.
5. Explain the reasons for your choices.

Mr A
Aged 60
Retired

Miss B
Aged 10
School student

Mr C
Aged 20
University student

Mrs D
Aged 38
Media Studies teacher

D *What styles of music and artistes might these people listen to?*

How styles of music develop

All current styles of popular music are linked to music from the past. For example, hip hop has its origins in jazz and blues music from the early 20th century. It can be traced even further back to the history of slavery in America, and from there to the dances and songs of West African story-tellers.

Blues

Born out of the hardships of a racially segregated society, blues was a combination of slave field songs with instruments such as the guitar and the piano.

Rhythm and blues (R&B)

Born in the late 1940s, in America, R&B was used to describe the combination of jazz and blues music by black American musicians.

Soul

Soul was created in the early 1960s, when R&B was combined with gospel music. Made popular by US record labels Stax and Motown.

Funk

Originated in the late 1960s when musicians blended soul, jazz and R&B into a new danceable form of music.

Hip hop

Born in the South Bronx in New York, MCs rapped over loops and samples from disco and funk beats, made by DJs using turntables as instruments.

Robert Johnson

Ray Charles

Aretha Franklin

James Brown

Jay Z

E *The evolution of hip hop*

Research activity

1 Choose one style of music to research.

a What are the conventions of the style of music?

b Explain how the style of music has changed.

c List five key artistes that represent the style of music. Explain the significance and importance of those artistes to this particular style of music.

Did you know ??????

Record labels do not always get it right. In 1962 a new group from Liverpool auditioned for Decca records. The head of Decca turned them down, saying 'Guitar groups are on the way out ...' The group was The Beatles!

6.2 Music posters

The promotion of music is rarely all about the music. What you see can sometimes be just as important as what you hear. The music industry uses visual media as a key part of its marketing strategy. The history of popular music is full of artistes who were promoted as much for their image as their musical talent.

How important is the image of an artiste?

- The visual image of a band or singer communicates important messages to the audience.
- Audiences often associate the look of an artiste to a style of music.
- Some audiences idolise bands and singers, and see them as sex symbols and fashion icons.

Music posters

In this section we are going to examine music posters. Music posters are a common component of any marketing strategy. They appear in magazines, on billboards, as fly-posters, on buses, in calendars and on bedroom walls. Some posters have become very famous, and iconic images have helped retain the popularity of existing and legendary artistes.

A *An iconic poster of Jim Morrison, lead singer of The Doors*

Objectives

To learn about the purpose of music posters.

To analyse music posters and the messages they communicate.

Discussion activity

How important is a strong visual image to the success of a band or singer?

Did you know ??????

Fly-posting is the act of placing advertising posters in illegal areas. Camden Borough Council in London once threatened to take Sony and BMG to court for illegal fly-posting.

All popular music posters are about promotion. They fall into three main categories:

- promotion of a single or album release
- promotion of a tour or live appearance
- general fan posters of an artiste or band.

Analysing a music poster

Most music posters are carefully constructed to communicate certain messages about the artiste. Images may consist of album cover artwork, photographs of the band or artiste, graphics and text. As a media studies student, your challenge is to deconstruct these posters and analyse the messages they contain. You also need to evaluate how the poster promotes the artiste.

Activity

Choose one of the posters shown.

Using the key questions, write an analysis of your chosen poster.

Key questions

You have chosen a music poster to analyse:

- Identify the type of poster and its purpose.
- How is the band or singer represented in the image?
- How is the music of the band or singer represented in the image?
- If the band or singer is absent, why?
- How are graphics used on the poster?
- How has the image been constructed?
- How are lighting and colour used in the poster?
- What are the main colours used in the poster? What are the connotations of the colours used?
- What symbols are used in the poster? What do they say about the artiste?
- Who do you think is the intended audience for the poster?
- How effective do you think the poster is at promoting the artiste?

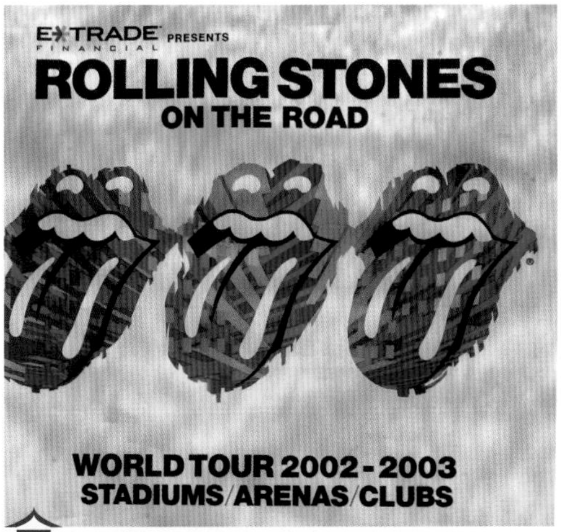

B *Rolling Stones tour poster*

C *White Stripes tour poster*

6.3 Music video

Since the 1980s and the arrival of music television, the video has been an important feature of music promotion. In the past, music video largely concentrated on the promotion of the single. Sometimes the video became as successful as the music. Michael Jackson's 14-minute video for *Thriller* was so popular that, at its peak, it was repeated twice an hour on **MTV**.

Today, new technologies have presented greater opportunities for video promotion, and while sales of singles have declined, the value of the music video is more important than ever.

Types of music video

There are three main categories of music video:

- **Narrative:** where the aim of the video is to tell a story. The story is often related to the lyrics of the song, which act as a sort of musical narration. The artistes often appear as actors in the video.
- **Performance:** where the artiste appears to perform the song. This is the most common type of video, and it is usually based on a recording of a live performance, or a heavily edited and constructed 'performance'.
- **Abstract:** where the video features an abstract interpretation of the music. The artiste may not actually appear in the video.

Objectives

To examine how the music industry uses video to promote its artistes and music.

To analyse music videos.

Activities

1 Make a list of all the ways you can access music videos.

2 How important do you think videos are in the promotion of music?

Key terms

MTV: Music TeleVision; MTV was launched in the USA in 1981.

A *Britney Spears shooting the music video for* Outrageous

Analysing a music video

Activities

3 In pairs, make a list of your five favourite music videos.

4 For each video, explain why you chose it for your list.

5 What do you think are the ingredients for a successful music video?

Did you know ??????

The 1975 promotional film for *Bohemian Rhapsody* by the British rock group Queen is regarded as the first modern music video.

Choose a music video to study

When analysing a music video, you will need to watch it a number of times. But before you watch it, get a copy of the lyrics and think about the meaning of the song. This will help you when you come to evaluate the video. Next, watch the video a few times and:

- Identify what type of video it is.
- Describe what happens in the video.
- Describe how the video has been constructed.

Constructing your analysis

- How is the song portrayed or interpreted in the video? How is the style of music represented in the video?
- How is the band or artiste represented in the video? What messages or impressions do you get about the artiste?
- How are editing and camera movement used in the video? How are lighting and colour used?
- What is the overall effect of the video? Does the video add to the song? Does the video help to sell the song?

Example

Here is an extract of a student's analysis of 'Back to Black' by Amy Winehouse:

Extract

Overall, this video is a narrative video. It tells the story of a funeral with Amy Winehouse acting as one of the people attending the funeral. The video cuts to Amy Winehouse singing the song while she is waiting for the funeral car. The video seems to be based in the 1960s, and you can tell this by fashions, cars and the black and white film. The retro/sixties theme is continued in the image of Amy Winehouse, with her beehive hairstyle and heavy eyeliner. The video seems to compare the end of a love affair to a funeral, and the black and white photography adds to this atmosphere of doomed love...

6.4 Case study – the Arctic Monkeys

Case study

The Arctic Monkeys

Name: Arctic Monkeys

Genre: Indie rock

Origin: Sheffield, UK

Formed: 2002

Record label: Domino

Objectives

To examine the success of the Arctic Monkeys and consider the band's impact on the music industry.

A *The Arctic Monkeys*

DIY success

The rise of the Arctic Monkeys has marked an important shift in the way artistes can achieve success in the music business. Traditionally, artistes have relied on getting signed to a record label which then promotes and markets them through the usual methods of radio airplay, television appearances and advertising. This process of record label discovery has become the basis for popular television programmes, such as *The X Factor* and *Pop Idol*.

By using the internet, the Arctic Monkeys have managed to turn this process on its head and achieve success without any of the old reliance on record companies to discover, launch and market their music.

The road to success

This is how they succeeded:

- The Arctic Monkeys built up a strong following through live performances.
- The band gave away free demo singles at gigs.
- Using MySpace, fans were able to download tracks for free and get gig information.
- The name 'Arctic Monkeys' began to spread on internet chatrooms.
- The band's demos began to sell in large numbers on Ebay.
- Then *NME (New Musical Express)*, BBC Radio 1 and XFM championed the band.
- The band eventually signed to the independent record label Domino.
- Media hype and a growing and loyal fan base helped build anticipation for the band's first official releases.

Success

Here are some of their achievements:

- The Arctic Monkeys's first album *Whatever People Say I Am, That's What I'm Not* was the fastest selling debut album ever (over 100 000 copies sold on its first day of release).
- The band's first two singles *I Bet You Look Good On The Dancefloor* and *When The Sun Goes Down* were UK Number 1 singles.
- The Arctic Monkeys won the 2006 Mercury Music Award, the 2006 Best British Breakthrough Act at the Brit Awards, and Best New Band and the Best Band at the *NME* awards.
- The Arctic Monkeys headlined Glastonbury in 2007.

B *How important are live performances?*

Discussion activities

1. What does the success of the Arctic Monkeys tell you about how the music business has changed?
2. What do you think was the most important factor that contributed to the success of the band?
3. Why might some other artistes welcome what has happened with the Arctic Monkeys?
4. Is this the end for the major record labels?

Extension activity

Research the success of a current popular artiste or band.

Explain how the artiste or band has been marketed.

Did you know ??????

Other artistes have used the internet to promote their music without record label involvement:

- US band Hawthorne sold 500 000 copies of their 2004 debut album *The Silence in Black and White*, by using MySpace to promote themselves.
- MySpace helped My Chemical Romance's 2004 album *Three Cheers for Sweet Revenge* to sell over 1 million copies.

6.5 Cross-media assignment: Part 1

Objectives

To look at how to produce your analysis for the cross-media assignment of the controlled assessment.

In this chapter, you have examined how the music industry uses different media to promote bands and artistes. In the previous topic you looked in detail at how the Arctic Monkeys used their fan base and the internet to promote themselves.

AQA GCSE media studies requires you to complete a cross-media assignment that analyses two promotional methods. You should try and aim for approximately 1000 words in length.

Explore the way in which one *band or artiste is represented and promoted across at least* two *different media, e.g. music video, radio or television appearances, magazine interviews or advertisements, internet sites.*

Choose one *print or web-based media text and* one *audio-visual media text.*

Step 1 Planning and research

- Choose a band or artiste that you know well or are interested in.
- Make sure you have access to a variety of promotional material. Remember, you need to compare *two* promotional methods: *one* print or web-based and *one* audio-visual media text.
- Find out all you can about the band or artiste.
- Listen to the band or artiste's music, visit their website and MySpace page, watch their videos, and look at their CD and poster artwork. Think about how they are being promoted.

Step 2 Choices

- Decide which two aspects of the promotional campaign you are going to analyse.
- You could look at two methods that promote the band or artiste in general, or narrow your focus to concentrate on analysing the promotion of a single or album.
- The print or web-based media text could include a magazine interview or advertisement or internet site.
- The audio-visual media text could include the video, a radio broadcast or a television appearance.

Step 3 Analysis of print or web-based text

- Identify the codes and conventions of your media text.
- Remember, the aim of the text is to promote the product. Look for all the messages and clues contained within the text.
- You may find it helpful to have a hard copy of the text, and to begin your analysis by highlighting the key features of the text.

Step 4 Analysis of the audio-visual media text

- Identify the codes and conventions of your media text.
- When studying moving image or an audio text you will need to revisit it a number of times to help you unpick all the features contained within it.
- As with Step 3, look closely for all the messages.
- If you are studying a video, try to print off some of the frames or stills. This may help you to focus your analysis.

links

You may wish to look at pages 34–35 and 76–77 for some guidance on analysing printed media.

A *Radio interviews are often part of a strategy to promote music*

Step 5 Comparison and evaluation

- Now you need to compare the texts you have chosen.
- How is the band or artiste represented in the texts you have studied?
- Explain the impact the texts would have on the target audience.
- How effective are these promotional texts?

6.6 Cross-media assignment: Part 2

As part of your cross-media study, AQA GCSE media studies requires you to produce a research and planning assignment.

Research and plan one *print or web-based or new media task and* one *audio-visual media task.*

The print or web-based or new media task can include:

...mock-up design for a magazine article, a print-based advert, a record company press release or a MySpace page promoting a band or artiste.

The audio-visual media task can include:

...a storyboard for a music video or a script for a television or radio interview promoting the same band or artiste.

In this assignment you will be required to:

- Devise a marketing campaign.
- Research and plan one print or web-based promotional text.
- Research and plan one audio-visual promotional text.
- Explain how your promotional material fits into your marketing campaign, and the impact it will have on your target audience.

The following assignment is designed for small groups of students.

Step 1 Planning and research

- You and your group represent a new independent record label. Come up with a name and logo for your record label.
- Imagine your company scouts have discovered a new artiste or band. Produce a band or artiste fact file that includes the name of the artiste(s), style of music, ages and so on.

Step 2 Creating the band

- Create a logo for the band or artiste. This will help to create an identity.
- Create a product or products for the band or artiste. These could include a single, album, tour, DVD release. Remember to try and choose suitable titles for your band or artiste.
- You may wish to collect or create photographs of your band or artiste. Think carefully about how their style of music might affect the way they look.

Step 3 Planning a marketing strategy

- Identify the target audience for your band or artiste.
- Produce a diagram to describe your target audience. Include their age, lifestyle, fashion, music taste, etc.
- Devise a marketing strategy that will sell the band or artiste to your target audience. Think about which magazines, radio stations and television shows you might wish to use. How important will the web be to your strategy?

Objectives

To look at how to approach the production task for the cross-media assignment of the controlled assessment.

A *Examples of band logos*

Step 4 Production

- Decide on *one* print or web-based promotional text and *one* audio-visual promotional text to produce.
- Think about how your two texts fit into your campaign. It is important that your two texts complement each other.
- Plan and produce your two texts. Remember, this is a pre-production task, so if you have chosen to produce a music video you need to complete a storyboard sheet.

Step 5 Presentation

- For your two promotional texts, present an explanation of their potential impact on your target audience.
- In your explanation, consider where and when your promotional material would appear. Explain your choices.

BAND FACT FILE

Name of band: Three Cheers

Origin: New Jersey, USA

Style of music: Pop (wholesome)

Band members: Stacey Lee (aged 20) – lead vocalist
Chelsie Jones (aged 20) – backing singer
Jack Lee (aged 22) – guitar
Marlon Arthey (aged 21) – keyboard
Gary Ortega (aged 24) – drums

Formed: 2008. Stacey and Jack are brother and sister, and the original members of the band.

Audience: Mainly girls aged 9 to 16, who are into wholesome pop music that has a catchy tune and a chorus that hooks you in.

Success to date: The band's first single reached Number 5 in the United States. They are hoping to make it big in the UK by launching their second song on the back of a Hollywood blockbuster.

B *Your band/artiste fact file might look something like this*

Did you know ??????

As a publicity stunt and to gain extra investment, Cambridge-based indie band Hamfatter appeared on BBC's *Dragon's Den*. As a result, entrepreneur Peter Jones decided to invest £75 000 in the band, and media interest rocketed following the band's television appearance.

links

You may wish to refer to pages 12–13 to help describe your audience.

For guidance on producing storyboards, see pages 54–55.

Summary

In this chapter you have studied:

- how music is promoted by record companies
- how music is categorised and marked to different audiences
- how to analyse music posters
- how to analyse music video
- the rise of the Arctic Monkeys
- how to produce the cross-media assignment based on music promotion.

7 Advertising and marketing

Objectives

- To look at definitions of advertising and marketing.
- To look at advertising agencies and advertising campaigns.

Key definitions

What is advertising?

Advertising is the practice of calling the public's attention to a product or a service. It usually takes the form of a declaration in newspapers and magazines; or on the radio and television; or on hoardings and bus shelters. These declarations are paid for.

Advertisements are:

- a form of communication that tries to encourage consumption of products or services
- creations and reinforcements of a brand image and a brand loyalty
- messages that often mix factual information with persuasion.

Opposing views on advertising

Those for

It is essential for economic growth. It can be used to inform, educate and even entertain.

Those against

It has become a public nuisance. It has increasingly invaded public spaces.

What is product placement

This is sometimes known as **covert advertising**. It happens when a product or brand is clearly visible or often referred to in a television programme or film.

Advertising agencies

Advertising agencies vary in size. They may be just one- or two-person businesses or multi-national organisations.

Interactive agencies may offer a mix of web design and development, and internet advertising and marketing.

Interactive agencies rose to prominence before the traditional advertising agencies fully embraced the internet. The most successful interactive agencies provide specialised advertising and marketing services for the **digital space**.

Key terms

Digital space: any multimedia-enabled electronic channel that an advertiser's message can be seen or heard from.

Integrated marketing communication: an attempt to ensure that information about a product or service is effectively distributed to the intended audience.

Promotional activities: activities which attempt to raise awareness of a product or service.

Starter activity

In small groups, make a list of three advertisements that appear in each of these media: newspapers, magazines, radio, television, hoardings and bus shelters.

Type 'advertising agencies' into a search engine to find out what agencies exist and the kind of work they do.

Agency departments

Advertising agencies tend to have creative, creative services, and accounts management departments.

The **creative department**, as you would expect, is responsible for making the advertisements. The department is divided into copywriters and art directors. Teams may be assembled on a permanent basis or they may be put together on a single project basis.

The **creative services department** comprises the staff who have contacts with people in associated industries. For example, they know people in the print industry and are able to negotiate production contracts.

The **accounts management department** contains the staff who meet with the clients to discuss their needs. They coordinate the activities of the other departments. They oversee completion of the product and the placement of the product at the end of the process.

Advertising campaigns

Advertising campaigns are a series of messages that share a single idea and theme. Together the messages make up an **integrated marketing communication**.

The driving force behind any advertising campaign is determining what has been called a **champion theme**. This establishes the tone for the individual advertisements that will be used. The campaign theme is the central message that will be communicated in the **promotional activities**. Campaign themes tend to be developed to be used over a prolonged period of time. But some of them are designed to be used only over a short period. This may be because market conditions have changed.

AQA Examiner's tip

Ask yourself: is advertising selling a product or is it selling you an image of yourself?

7.1 Textual analysis

Denotation and connotation

Objectives

To look at how we might analyse print advertisements.

When we try to understand advertisements, we use a method known as textual analysis. This explores what is actually in front of us and what we bring to the advertisements from our own experience.

What is in front of us is called the **denotation**.

What we bring to the analysis is known as **connotation**.

The denotation is made up of media language. In turn, this is constructed by:

- the layout of the advertisement
- the type of camera shot used
- the *mise-en-scène*
- the colours used in the advertisement
- the font(s) used
- the language used.

The layout of the advertisement

A lot of time is spent arranging the content of advertisements to maximise the impact upon audiences. See pages 110–111 to discover how key elements of an advertisement are placed in positions that our eye is drawn to first.

The type of camera shot used

The intention of advertising is to draw attention to a product. It therefore follows that a close-up shot is more likely to do this than a long shot. The way that focusing is used is also important in attracting the audience's attention.

The mise-en-scène

This is a French term. It is usually used when we are talking about cinema, but increasingly when referring to any visual image. It means, 'put in the scene'. It refers to anything that can be seen by the camera. It is also used to describe the technical codes of lighting, camera angles, type of shot and focusing.

The colours used in the advertisement

Relying on denotation, colours are used to create moods and to suggest particular audience reactions.

The font(s) used

Different font sizes, styles and colours are used to convey different messages and to provoke different audience reactions.

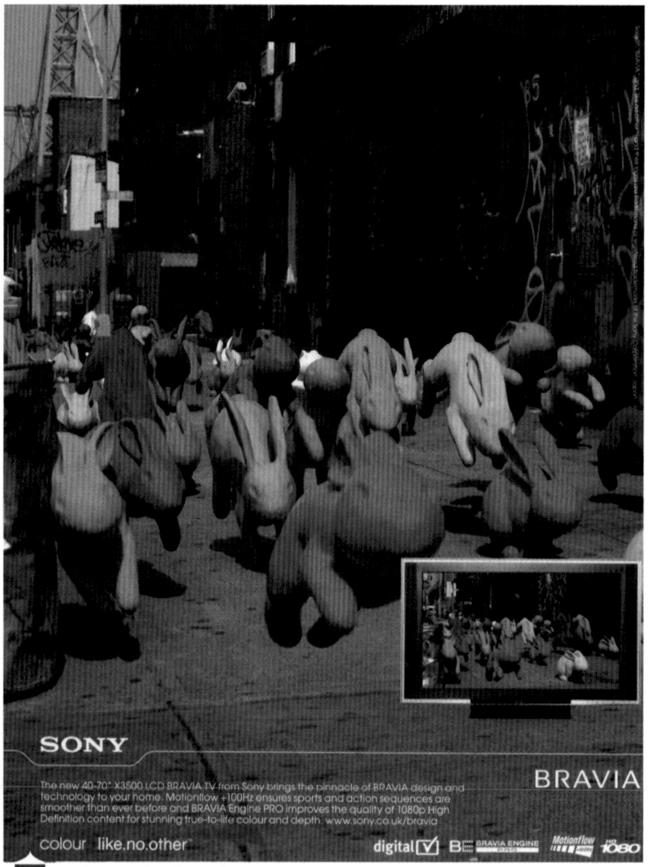

A *Why might this advertisement for a television use colour so strongly?*

The language used

The language often appears to be giving the audience factual information. At the same time it attempts to encourage emotional responses. Sentence structure tends to be short and punchy.

Look at the advertisement in **A**.

- What is the denotation?
- What are the connotations?
- What can be said about the *mise-en-scène*?
- What can be said about the layout?
- What is being advertised (think beyond the product to consider lifestyle and aspiration)?
- What assumptions are made about the audience?
- What does the whole image tell you about institutions and their values?
- Is the advertisement factual or persuasive?

Consider these phrases:

- Colour like no other
- Pinnacle of Bravia design and technology
- Bravia Engine PRO
- Smoother than ever before
- Stunning true-to-life colour.

- What sort of language is being used (suggestive/emotive/scientific)?
- Can the claims be substantiated?
- Can the claims be tested?
- Can the company be taken to court for not doing 'what it says on the tin'?

Activity

Deconstruct the advertisement shown in **B**, using the skill and understanding that you have developed:

- What is it selling?
- How is it selling it?
- How does it fit into a modern context?
- What does it assume about the readers' existing knowledge?
- What is it saying about representation?

B *Does this advertisement belong to a particular genre?*

7.2 Analysing a print advertisement

A *This advertisement for Kellogg's appeared in the* Radio Times, *30 August to 5 September 2008*

Objectives

To analyse a print advertisment, using denotation and connotation.

Did you know ??????

The eye is naturally drawn to the lighter areas of an image. This is why the white font has been used in the Kellogg's advertisement.

Denotation

Looking at advertisement **A**:

- We have a rectangular image in a portrait format.
- The background of the image is feathered vertically from a saturated yellow to white.
- In the top left, leading to the top right, with perspective added, we have a bordered rectangle. Bursting out of the upper border of this rectangle is a representation of a cockerel.
- In the right of the rectangle, in a bold red font outlined in white and to which perspective has been added, is the instruction: 'Wake up to breakfast'.
- In the top right-hand corner the instruction continues: 'with Kellogg's'. The brand name is stylised and outlined in white to lift it off the background. In a plain, bold red font the instruction becomes a challenge: 'and see if you can …'
- Below, occupying the width of the page, presented in bold and appearing four times the size of the plain font above, the challenge becomes: 'perform better'.

The image is divided horizontally by the flourish of a red banner which widens as it approaches the right-hand-side of the page.

This division makes everything above the line into a masthead. Below the line we have the 'important information':

- We have a photograph of a woman wearing a red tracksuit top and holding a white bowl of what appears to be a breakfast cereal. She is smiling and appears to have a healthy complexion.
- In the bottom left, in a plain black font, is a signature and title.
- Finally, we are instructed to: 'Put yourself to the test at www.kelloggs.co.uk/wakeup'.

Connotation

The colour scheme

- Yellows and greens suggest the natural; the environmentally friendly.
- Reds traditionally suggest danger, but here might be suggesting the blood flow which is required for us to perform.
- The white suggests purity.

The layout

- We read text from left to right. We scan images from right to left.
- In the most important position, the top right-hand side, is the brand name.
- Also to the right-hand side is the photograph.

The language

- 'Research shows' is an attempt to appear to be a scientific report. We are not told what research or who conducted it.
- We are instructed and challenged: by scientists? by Kellogg's scientists?

The audience

The advertisement appeared in the *Radio Times* whose primary audience is probably middle-class parents or grand parents who are concerned about the development of their offspring.

They are also aware of the necessity of a healthy lifestyle for performance in a competitive world.

The timing of this placement

The advertisement was placed at the end of August 2008, the end of the Beijing Olympics.

At first sight it therefore has only a limited life span. But, since attention to the Olympics shifted from Beijing to London it may well be used as part of an ongoing campaign leading up to 2012.

Celebrity endorsement

Dame Kelly Holmes wins Olympic medals. She also eats Kellogg's (although we do not actually see her eating). Do you want to succeed? Shouldn't you be eating Kellogg's?

kerboodle!

7.3 Analysing a moving-image advertisement

A key factor in nearly every advertising campaign will be the moving-image advertisements that appear on television or the internet. Advertising agencies will attempt to achieve synergy by placing the product on as many media platforms as possible – radio, television, magazines, newspapers and the internet – to ensure maximum exposure to the public so that the product cannot be ignored.

Objectives

- To learn how to analyse a moving-image advertisement.
- To look at how a cross-media campaign is created.

Case study

Citroën C4 transformer campaign

Analysis of 'Staying Alive' advertisement

The campaign started on television in 2005, with a stunning but very simple advertisement in which a Citroen car transformed into a robot and danced. The special effects were striking but the content of the advertisement was very simple. A media-wide campaign was launched with the robot later seen ice-skating, going through a warm-up routine and, in 2008, strutting through the streets of New York City.

A *A still, from the advert of the 'robotic' Citroën*

Activity

1 Watch the whole Citroën C4 advertisement.

a Apply denotation and connotation to three aspects of the advertisement, including the voiceover.

b What does the advertisement *tell* you about the car?

c How does the advertisement *sell* the car?

Key terms

Parody: an imitation.

Intertextuality: where one media text makes reference to another.

Location

New York City is one of the most recognisable places in the world. The Citroën advertisement uses iconography to quickly establish the location: yellow cabs, skyscrapers, battered-looking subway trains and the Brooklyn Bridge. Why New York City? Because it's seen as a centre of culture and technology. The advertisements want the Citroën car to appear stylish and modern – so where better?

Denotation/connotation

There are dozens of examples where this could be applied. Here is one:

- Denotation – the robot is silver in colour.
- Connotation – silver is associated with modern cars, technology and wealth.

Music

The advertisement uses the Bee Gees' 1978 hit 'Staying Alive', which older viewers will recognise from its first release; but it's one of those cheesy favourites that probably everyone has heard of. If not, it's a very catchy tune and will soon appeal. The music has been given a hip hop makeover to appear more modern. The song 'fits' because of the dancing and a link with the campaign slogan: 'Alive With Technology'.

B *Another still: the advertisement draws the audience in with its well-known and catchy tune*

Intertextuality

'Staying Alive' was a hit record but, perhaps more importantly, the title of the sequel to the film *Saturday Night Fever* in which John Travolta performed many famous dance sequences. By offering a **parody** of the film (there is one famous scene where Travolta struts through the streets full of confidence) the advertisement catches the attention and pleases the viewers who remember the earlier film. If you're not familiar with *Saturday Night Fever*, you can still enjoy the advertisement. Another example of **intertextuality** is that the robot does the 'moonwalk', which is a reference to Michael Jackson. It doesn't really matter that the 'moonwalk' didn't appear in *Saturday Night Fever*.

Billboards

As part of the same campaign, the robot replaces the Statue of Liberty (which is in New York) and is seen striking a *Saturday Night Fever* pose!

7.4 Cross-media assignment: part 1

Objectives

To look at how to produce your analysis for the cross-media assignment of the controlled assessment

In this chapter, you have examined how advertising institutions use different media platforms to promote goods and services.

AQA GCSE Media Studies requires candidates to produce a cross-media assignment that analyses two advertisements for the same product or service across two media platforms. You should try to aim for a length of approximately 1000 words.

> "Compare the impact and effectiveness of **two** advertisements for the same product or service across **two** media platforms."

Step 1 Planning and research

- Choose an advertisement that you know well or are interested in. You may choose a recent advertisement, or a non-contemporary advertisement.
- Make sure you have access to examples from the advertising campaign. Remember you will need to analyse two advertisements for the same product or service across two media platforms.
- Find out all you can about the advert. The Web is full of sites offering background information and trivia about different advertising campaigns.

A *You need to compare two advertisements for the same product or service across two media platforms*

Step 2 Choices

- Decide which two examples of the advertising campaign you are going to analyse.
- The platforms you could choose from include: television, radio, internet and print media.

Step 3 Analysis of advertisements

- Key question: Explain how the advertisements attempt to persuade the target audience to buy the product/service.

In your answer you should consider the following:

- What are the codes and conventions of your media text?
- Using technical terminology, explain the layout, narrative or content of the advertisement.
- Who are the target audience for the advertisement?
- What does the advertisement say about the product?
- What media representations are contained in the advertisement?
- What is the impact of media representations in the advertisement?
- How does the advertisement make the product/service attractive to the target audience?

Analysing print-based advertisements

- Remember to look at every component of the advertisement. Examine images, text, colour, composition and typography. What are the connotations of these features?
- You may wish to look back at section 2.7. This section gives some guidance about analysing print-based media.
- You may find it helpful to have a hard copy of the text, and to begin your analysis by text marking.

Analysing audio-visual advertisements

- Remember to look at every component of the advertisement. Examine the mise-en-scène, lighting, editing, diegetic and non-diegetic sound, and titles. What are the connotations of these features?
- When studying moving image or an audio text you will need to revisit the text a number of times to help you unpick all the messages and connotations contained within the text.
- You may wish to refer back to section 3.6. This section gives some guidance about analysing moving image and audio texts.
- If you are studying a moving image advertisement, try to print off some of the frames or stills. This may help you focus your analysis.

AQA *Examiner's tip*

www.thinkbox.tv/ contains many examples of recent advertisements including useful background information and campaign evaluations.

links

See pages 106–107 to find out what departments exist in an advertising agency.

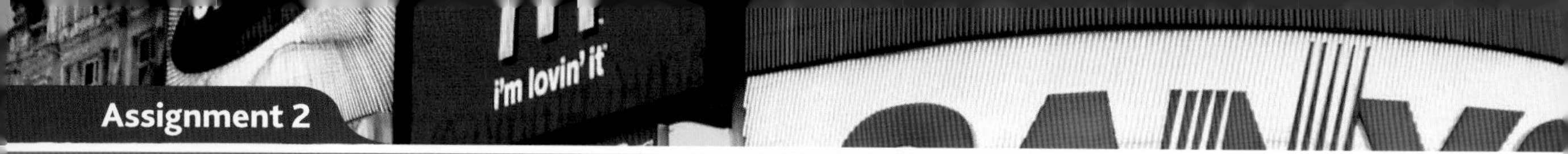

7.5 Cross-media assignment: part 2

As part of your cross-media study, AQA GCSE Media Studies requires candidates to produce a research and planning assignment.

Research and plan **one** print- or web-based/new media advertisement and **one** audio-visual advertisement.

The print or web-based/new media assignment can include:

> *...mock-up design for an advertisement for a magazine, newspaper or billboard.*

The audio-visual advertisement can include:

> *...a storyboard for a television or viral advertisement or a script for a radio advertisement for the same product.*

In this task you will need to:

- research and plan an advertising campaign
- demonstrate flair and creativity
- use appropriate forms and conventions
- skilfully present two planned production assignments that clearly complement each other.

Step 1 Planning and research

- First decide on the product/brand you are going to advertise. (Your teacher may decide this for you.)
- Identify an audience for your product.
- Create a profile of your target audience.
- Select two media platforms for your advertising campaign. Remember one must be print-based, and the other must be audio-visual.
- Record your ideas on a planning sheet.

Step 2 Creating the campaign

- Decide on the USP of your product.
- Decide what messages about your product you want to include in your advertising campaign.
- Create a tag line to appear in your campaign
- Think about how your two advertisements fit into your campaign. It is important that your two texts complement each other.

Step 3 Production

- Produce your print-based advertisement. Remember this is a pre-production task, so it is acceptable to produce a mock of your design.
- If appropriate try to include original photography in your advertisement.
- Produce your audio-visual advert. Remember this is a pre-production task, so choose either a storyboard for television/internet or a script for a radio advertisement.

Objectives

To look at how to produce the production task assignment for the cross-media assessment.

links

Refer to pages 28 and 29 for examples of audience profiles.

Key terms

USP (unique selling point): an aspect of a product that makes it distinct from similar products.

Tag line: a memorable slogan or phrase that will sum up the tone of a brand or product.

Did you know ??????

The cost of buying a 30 second advertising slot in 2010 during the televising of the Super Bowl cost $2.6 million dollars.

A *You must consider your audience and market very carefully*

Step 4 Presentation

- For your advertising campaign present an explanation of your advertisements' appeal and impact on your target audience.
- In your explanation consider where and when your advertisements would appear. Explain your choices.
- Explain how your two advertisements are connected and representative of a cross-media campaign.

Summary

In this chapter you have studied:

- the definitions of advertising and marketing
- the structure of advertising agencies and advertising campaigns
- how to analyse print advertisements
- how to analyse moving image advertisements
- how to produce the cross-media assignment based on advertising and marketing.

8 Film promotion

Objectives

To learn about how films are marketed to the public.

To examine how different media platforms are used by the film industry.

Box office hits

Titanic is the highest **grossing** film of all time. Released in 1997 and produced by 20th Century Fox, it made a staggering $1 842 913 795 at the box office. At the time it was also the most expensive movie ever produced, costing over $200 million. What made this film so successful?

A *The highest grossing films of all time*

Rank	Movie name	Studio(s)	Worldwide gross	Year
1	*Titanic*	20th Century Fox/Paramount	$1 842 913 795	1997
2	*The Lord of the Rings: The Return of the King*	New Line Cinema	$1 129 000 000	2003
3	*Pirates of the Caribbean: Dead Man's Chest*	Walt Disney Company/Buena Vista	$1 066 179 725	2006
4	*The Dark Knight*	Warner Bros	$992 272 339	2008
5	*Harry Potter and the Philosopher's Stone*	Warner Bros	$976 475 550	2001

As you will see from table **A**, Hollywood studios in America dominate the film industry. The main aim of Hollywood studios is to make money. However, the reasons behind a smash hit at the box office are varied and complex. First, the cost of the film production has to be recouped, and it is estimated that a film has to make at least two-and-a-half times its production costs in order to go into profit.

There are many ingredients that can contribute to the success of a film. However, a high budget promotion campaign, famous cast, and a popular **genre** do not necessarily ensure financial success. The *Adventures of Pluto Nash* (Warner Brothers, 2000) starring Eddie Murphy had a budget of $100 million but only made $4.4 million at the box office. As you can see, the movie business can be both a very profitable and a very risky business.

Marketing the film

One of the key factors in determining the success or failure of any film is the marketing campaign. Selling the film to the target audience involves generating publicity, expectation and interest.

Key terms

Grossing: refers to money made at the box office.

Genre: from the French meaning 'type'. When we talk about a genre of film, we might refer to science fiction, romantic comedy or several other 'types' of film.

Turkey: a film that performs very badly at the box office.

A film marketing campaign usually consists of three parts:

- **Advertising:** paid for by the studio to sell the film to the target audience, e.g. the film poster.
- **Publicity:** not paid for directly by the studio, but used to create interest in the film, e.g. an interview given by one of the stars of the film.
- **Tie-ins:** authorised products designed to generate additional publicity and income for the studio and film.

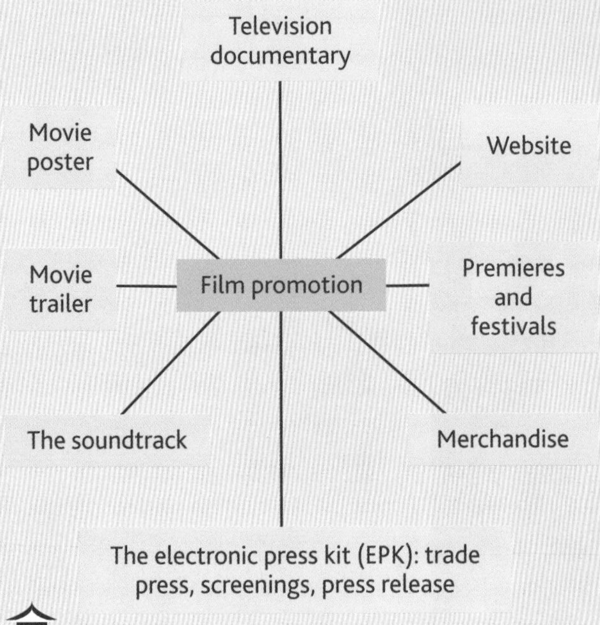

B *Which of these areas are publicity, advertising and tie-ins?*

Starter activity

1. Research each method of film promotion shown in diagram **B**. For each method, explain how it is used to promote the film.
2. Discuss with your partner which ideas are the most effective promotional method and why.

Did you know ??????

While *Titanic* was a massive success, a major British **turkey** was *Raise the Titanic*. Produced in 1980, it was a major flop at the box office. Costing what was then a huge $35 million, the producer, Lew Grade, famously remarked that 'it would have been cheaper to lower the Atlantic'.

8.1 Genre and the film industry

A *What genre is this film?*

B *Can you guess the genre of this film?*

Objectives

To learn how films are classified by genre.

Activities

1. Make a list of your five favourite films.
2. Look at your list, which genres do the films represent?
3. Working in groups, compare your choices. Which genres are the most popular in your class?

Genre

Understanding the genre of a film is very important when examining film promotion. Different films have different stories, but nearly all of them fit into certain categories known as genre. Horror, war, romantic comedy and action are all examples of genre. We, as the audience, are quick to recognise genre, and will have certain expectations about the content and **narrative** of that type of film.

The clues to reading genre are the conventions. Look again at the film stills above. Each picture contains key conventions that we as the audience would associate with a particular genre.

Key terms

Narrative: the story – a sequence of events.

Sub-genre: an identifiable sub-class from a larger film genre. For example, a martial arts film is a type of action film.

C *Does this film look like a thriller or a romantic comedy?*

Activity

4 Working in pairs, choose eight popular genres and create a table like the one below:

Genre	Conventions	Film titles
Action	Explosions, fight scenes, chase sequence, hero, villain	*Indiana Jones and the Kingdom of the Crystal Skull* *Casino Royale* *The Bourne Identity* *Die Hard* *Mission Impossible*

Try to include at least five conventions and five film titles that represents each genre.

Choose one genre from your table. Can you identify any related **sub-genres**? Name any actors or directors who have specialised in that genre.

Genre and marketing

Genre is a powerful tool for the film industry. Producers look carefully at which genres perform well at the box office, and often choose to finance films that have similarities to recent successes. The film industry knows that certain audiences will be attracted to certain types of film. Therefore, publicity material will usually have a clear sense of genre and will be carefully targeted at an appropriate audience.

Extension activity

1 Make a list of current film titles that are popular at the cinema.

a What does your list tell you about the popularity of certain genres? Why do you think these genres are currently popular?

b What sort of audiences are attracted to those genres?

8.2 Film posters

Types of film posters

One of the core elements of any film promotion is the film poster. Essentially there are three types of film poster:

- **The teaser poster:** this will be used in the initial publicity for the film, often well before the release of the actual film. The purpose of the teaser poster is to build up interest and expectation for the film. The teaser poster often gives little information about the actual plot, to 'tease' the audience.
- **The main poster:** this poster is usually dominated by a single image or collection of images from the film. Key written information is also included. Film posters may be altered during the lifetime of the film to keep the marketing campaign on-going.
- **DVD release poster:** produced to encourage the audience to own the film. The poster may highlight elements of the film unseen at the cinema, such as extended versions or a director's cut.

Objectives

- To understand the diferent types of film poster.
- To look at the conventions of film posters.
- To learn how to analyse film posters.

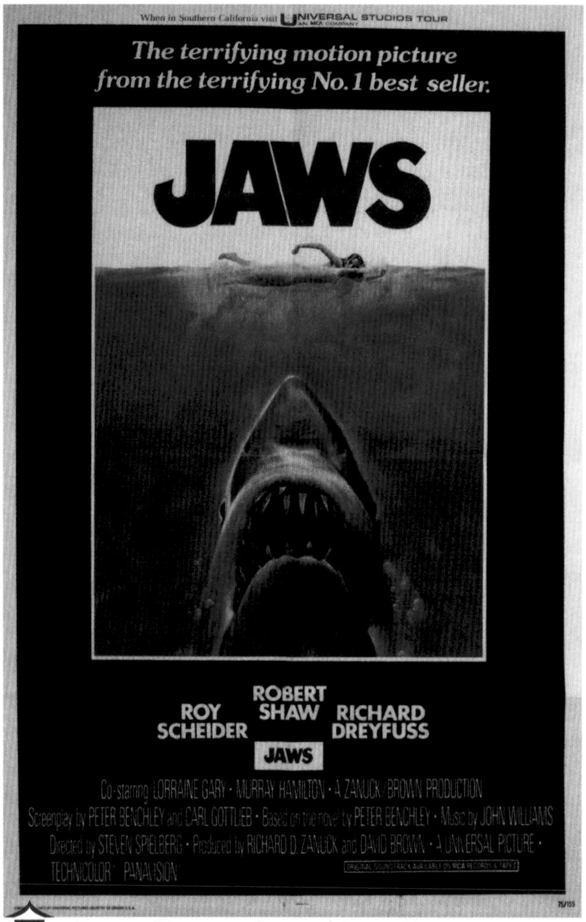

A *The main film poster for* Jaws*, directed by Steven Spielberg*

B *This film was nominated for seven Oscars*

C *The main film poster for this British action comedy*

D *A poster for one of the films in the* Pirates of the Caribbean *series*

What are the features of a film poster?

You will see film posters everywhere. They are displayed in the cinema foyer, placed in newspapers and magazines, pasted on billboards and can even be spotted on the sides of buses. The same images often appear later on the DVD cover, items of merchandise and the soundtrack CD. All this advertising costs large amounts of money, so production companies put a lot of effort into creating an effective design that will sell the film to the target audience.

Film posters

- Title of the film – prominent and clear
- One or more image from the film to convey genre, character and setting
- Tag line – a catchy phase or slogan about the film
- Names of the actors
- Name of the director
- A quote from a review
- Awards given to the film
- The name of the studio and the production company

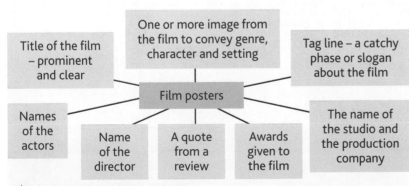

E *The features of film posters*

Activities

Here are some famous tag lines. Can you guess the film and genre?

1. 'The greatest fairy tale never told.'
2. 'There are 3.7 trillion fish in the ocean. They're looking for one.'
3. 'Protecting the Earth from the scum of the universe.'
4. 'An adventure 65 million years in the making.'
5. 'A long time ago in a galaxy far, far away.'
6. 'Mr Black. Accept no substitutes.'
7. 'Prepare to be blown out of the water.'
8. 'The Legend comes to Life.'

How to read a film poster

Film posters contain a number of messages about the film, through both the text and the imagery.

As media studies students you need to be able to read and explain these messages.

Analysing *3:10 to Yuma*

3:10 to Yuma is a Western. Released in 2007, it starred Russell Crowe and Christian Bale. In this exercise we are going to look for the clues and messages within the poster that help sell the film.

The actors have equal billing, so their names are placed at the same level on the poster.

Russell Crowe and Christian Bale are famous A-list stars. Their names are placed at the top of the poster because they are key selling points of the film.

The director's name is included but is not emphasised because his name is not a major selling point of the film.

'3:10' is the largest text on the poster, and different-sized lettering is used to draw attention to the title. The image of the clock helps stress the significance of time to the narrative of the film.

A *Film poster for* 3:10 to Yuma

What are the unique selling points of *3:10 to Yuma*?

- Fans of the Western genre will be attracted by this poster: there is a sense of drama and conflict in the poster, as well as many traditional Western conventions.
- The film stars Russell Crowe and Christian Bale: both actors are successful Hollywood stars and fans of these actors will be attracted to the film.
- The director (James Mangold) also directed *Walk the Line*: people who enjoyed that film may want to watch this film. *Walk the Line* was critically acclaimed and the audience may expect a similar quality from this film.

The 'aged' appearance of the poster helps emphasise the historical setting of the Western.

The choice of fonts and colour scheme are all associated with old-fashioned 'wanted' posters. This is another association with the American West. Old fashioned graphic swirls are also included for a similar effect.

The gun, the American steam train, and the character's costume are all conventions of the Western genre. These conventions establish the film both historically and geographically.

Reference to *Walk the Line* – a critically acclaimed film about the life of the singer Johnny Cash – the production company is using the director's association with an earlier successful film as a selling point for this film. The text is vertical, thus distancing itself from messages about the actual narrative of *3:10 to Yuma*.

The image suggests violence and conflict, as the character is standing in the path of the oncoming train.

The tag line is a play on the saying 'time waits for no man'. Here it waits for one man, thus emphasising the significance and power of the main character. Also, the reference to time is a further link to the role of time in the title and narrative.

The low-angle shot emphasises the stature and power of the main character. Is the main character a hero or a villain? He appears to be a gunslinger but is also shown in a heroic pose, standing up to the oncoming train. This confusion about the nature of the main character is one of the themes of the film.

Institutional information is produced in small print because it is not a selling point of the film.

Activities

1. Choose one of the film posters illustrated in the previous topic.
2. Analyse the content of the poster.
3. What are the unique selling points of that film and how are they communicated in the poster?
4. Overall, how effective do you think the film poster is at promoting the film?

AQA *Examiner's tip*

When analysing a media text, remember that someone has carefully created the text for a purpose. Your challenge is to try to unpick and explain all their ideas.

8.3 Film trailers

Types of film trailer

The film trailer is another essential element of any film marketing campaign. The aim of the trailer, like the film poster, is to build up expectation and interest with the audience. However the trailer, through sound and moving image, can convey the atmosphere and excitement of the film. The trailer itself consists of short clips that convey elements of the narrative and highlight the selling points of the film. The trailer will be shown in cinemas, on the internet and on television.

There are three types of film trailer:

- **The teaser trailer:** a shortened version of the trailer, shown well in advance of the film's release date. The trailer's aim is to 'tease' the audience and whet their appetite for the film.
- **The theatrical trailer:** usually shown a few weeks before the release date.
- **The DVD trailer:** mainly shown on television and the internet in advance of the DVD release.

What are the conventions of film trailers?

The trailer is a highly polished advert for the film. While the content of trailers may vary greatly, most will include certain key information:

- **Genre:** the trailer will clearly establish the genre to attract the target audience.
- **Plot:** almost like a shortened version of the film, they often follow a three-act structure. Part 1 establishes the storyline, Part 2 represents the dramatic development of the story, and Part 3 shows elements of the climax of the film.
- **Short clips:** of dialogue, action and drama.
- **Voice-over:** this is used to help the audience further understand the film. Certain types of voices are used to complement the tone of the film.
- **Music:** this helps establish the mood of the film and the drama of the trailer.
- **Cast:** popular and successful actors are often a major selling point of a film. If the film includes popular actors they will be a prominent feature of the trailer.
- **Director:** if the director is well known, or has made other successful films, his or her name may feature in the trailer.
- **The title:** this often appears at the end of the trailer.
- **The studio:** trailers will include the studio logo, often at the beginning or the end of a trailer.

Objectives

To understand the different types of film trailer.

To look at the conventions of film trailers.

To learn how to analyse film trailers.

Did you know ??????

Many trailers are produced before the actual film is completed. Sometimes special scenes are produced for the trailer that are not included in the actual film. The trailer for *Spiderman* (2002) included a whole chase sequence involving a helicopter being caught in a giant web between the Twin Towers in New York. Following the 2001 terrorist attacks this was pulled from the cinemas.

Activity

1 Think of a trailer you have seen recently:

a Where did you see the trailer?

b Did the trailer make you want to see the film?

Key terms

Diegetic sound: a sound that we might expect to hear in a particular scene.

Non-diegetic sound: a sound that does not normally belong in a particular scene.

High-key lighting: refers to any scene with a low lighting ratio. The lack of shadows and bright light often imply an upbeat mood; often used in comedies.

Low-key lighting: refers to any scene with a high lighting ratio. It is often used in horror films to create a shadowy atmosphere.

How to read a film trailer

The film trailer is an advert for the film. It has been carefully edited and produced to interest and attract the target audience. As media studies students you need to be able to unpick the trailer and explain its construction and appeal.

You need to base your analysis on four main areas: sound, use of lighting and colour, use of camera, editing.

Sound

Listen carefully to the audio track:

- What kind of music is used?
- What is the effect of the music?
- What type of voice-over is used?
- What is the effect of the voice-over?
- How are **diegetic** and **non-diegetic** sounds used?

Use of lighting and colour

- How is **high-key lighting** or **low-key lighting** used in the trailer?
- How is colour and tone used in the trailer?

Use of camera

- How are different shots used in the trailer?
- How are different angles used in the filming of the trailer?
- How is camera movement used in the trailer?

Editing

- What types of edits are included in the trailer?
- What is the effect of these edits?
- What does the pace of the trailer tell you about the film?

A *Low-key lighting*

B *A close-up shot*

AQA Examiner's tip

To help focus on certain aspects of a trailer:

- Listen to the trailer with the visuals turned off.
- Watch the trailer with the sound turned down.
- Pause the trailer. Watch it scene by scene.

Activity

2 Choose a current film trailer to study.

You will need to watch the trailer two or three times.

Complete a short written analysis of the film trailer. In your analysis, include:

- the name of the film
- the genre of the film
- the film's target audience
- a description of the narrative of the trailer
- the unique selling points of the film and state how they are highlighted in the trailer
- a paragraph analysing the use of sound in the trailer
- a paragraph analysing the use of lighting and colour in the trailer
- a paragraph analysing the use of the camera in the filming of the trailer
- a paragraph analysing the editing used in the trailer
- an overall conclusion on how effective the trailer is at promoting the film.

kerboodle!

8.4 Case study – *The Dark Night*

The Dark Knight

The Dark Knight was produced by Warner Brothers and released in 2008. It follows the recent popular trend in super hero films and is a sequel to 2005's *Batman Begins*. As the big budget blockbuster for summer 2008, the film benefited from a huge pre-release, cross-media, marketing campaign.

Objectives

To examine the marketing campaign behind *The Dark Knight*.

Viral marketing

Warner Brothers employed a company called '42 Entertainment' to begin a **viral marketing** campaign. In 2007 the company set up a website that featured the fictional political campaign of Harvey Dent (a character from the film). A vandalised version of the website called *I Believe in Harvey Dent Too* was also produced, where fans' emails slowly removed pixels to reveal the image of the Joker.

Key terms

Viral marketing: marketing that encourages people to pass on marketing messages through emails and texts.

The teaser poster and trailer

Warner Brothers produced a number of posters to advertise the film. Teaser posters were used to build-up expectation for the film, and the tag line 'why so serious' was taken up by the viral campaign. The teaser trailer was first shown alongside screenings of *I Am Legend*, as well as on the official website.

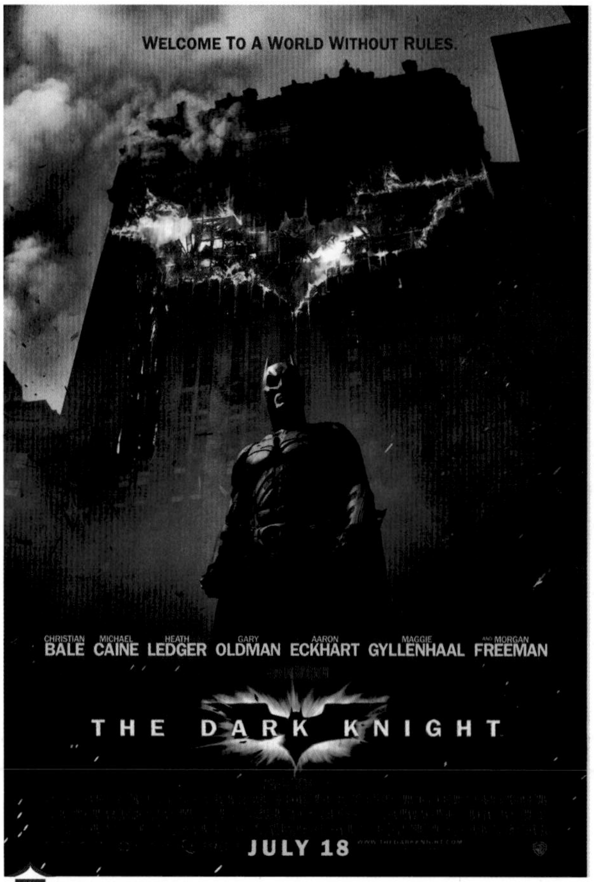

A The Dark Knight *film poster*

B The Dark Knight *teaser poster*

Tie-ins and publicity

The American toy maker Mattel has produced a range of games and toys to tie in with the film. These include action figures, card games and costumes. Other companies involved in product tie-ins include: Dominos, French Connection, Burger King, Nokia and Microsoft Xbox. In America *The Dark Knight* roller coaster opened at Six Flags Great Adventure theme park. At the 2008 British Grand Prix, the Toyota Formula One team raced with a special livery featuring the Batman insignia.

C *The Batmobile visits the British Grand Prix to promote* The Dark Knight

Controversy

The BBFC awarded a 12A rating to the film, which allows 12 year olds to watch the film unaccompanied, while younger children can watch the film with an adult. The violence in the film has caused controversy in the media, as many argue that its content was unsuitable for young children. The scenes of knife violence were particularly criticised, as it came at a time of growing public concern about knife crime in the UK.

In January 2008, Australian actor Heath Ledger was found dead at his home in Manhattan. Media interest in the death of the actor has led to speculation about a link with his performance as the demonic Joker in *The Dark Knight*, which reportedly left him unable to sleep.

Hillbilly Heroin killed Heath

E *Headline from the* Sun *(6 February 2008)*

Activities

1. Find out more about the viral marketing campaign for *The Dark Knight*. Try visiting www.whysoserious.com
2. How did the viral marketing campaign generate interest and expectation for the film?
3. Explain how tie-ins and publicity help the success of a film like *The Dark Knight*.
4. Collect images of a range of *The Dark Knight* products.
5. How do you think the controversy that surrounded *The Dark Knight* affected the popularity of the film?
6. How important do you think the BBFC rating is to the success of a film?

Growing anger at Batman's 12A rating

D *Batman in the news,* Daily Mail *(6 August 2008)*

kerboodle!

8.5 Cross-media assignment: part 1

Objectives

To look at how to produce your analysis for the cross-media assignment of the controlled assessment.

You have just examined how the film industry uses different areas of the media to promote a new film. In the previous topic you looked in detail at how Warner Brothers promoted *The Dark Knight*. AQA GCSE Media Studies requires you to produce a cross-media assignment that analyses two promotional methods. You should try to aim for approximately 800 words in length.

Compare the impact and effectiveness of two *promotional methods used by* one film, *e.g. poster; cinema, television or viral trailer; web page; magazine article; television interview.*

Choose one *print or web-based media text and* one *audio-visual media text.*

Step 1 Planning and research

- Choose a film that you know well or are interested in. You may choose to study a new release or a film that has been out for some time.
- Make sure you have access to a variety of promotional material. Remember you need to compare *two* promotional methods, *one* print or web-based media text and *one* audio-visual media text.
- Find out all you can about that film. The web is full of sites offering background information and trivia about different films.
- Watch the film. This will help you understand and evaluate the promotional campaign.

Step 2 Choices

- Decide which two aspects of the promotional campaign you are going to analyse.
- The print- or web-based media text could include: the film poster, website, magazine advert.
- The audio-visual media text could include the trailer, radio advert, viral trailer.

Step 3 Analysis of print or web-based text

- Identify the codes and conventions of your media text.
- Remember the aim of the text is to promote the film. Look for all the messages and clues contained within the text.
- How are the unique selling points highlighted in the text?
- You may find it helpful to have a hard copy of the text, and to begin your analysis by marking up the text.

Step 4 Analysis of the audio-visual media text

- Identify the codes and conventions of your media text.
- When studying moving image or an audio text you will need to revisit it a number of times to help you unpick all the features contained in the text.
- As with Step 3, look closely for all the messages and unique selling points.
- If you are studying a trailer, try to print off some of the frames or stills. This may help you focus your analysis.

Step 5 Comparison and evaluation

- Now you need to compare the texts you have studied.
- How is the film represented in the texts you have studied?
- Explain the impact the texts would have on the target audience.
- How effective are these promotional texts?

Example

Here is an example of a student's analysis about the use of sound in the film trailer for *The Lord of the Rings: The Fellowship of the Ring*.

The trailer begins with low non-diegetic sound. This helps set the dark tone of the trailer. The voice-over is that of Ian Mackellan, who plays Gandalf the Wizard. The voice-over gives the background of the story and there is also the distant sound of a voice singing in the background. Occasional discordant non-diegetic sounds are used to add to the tension. The whole atmosphere is of fear and suspense. The trailer then puts together different clips of dialogue from the film, featuring the key characters. Diegetic sounds accompany the clips along with dramatic music. The music then dies away, drawing attention to a particularly suspenseful part of the film when the characters hear something moving in the depths of the old Dwarfish Kingdom. The trailer ends with more dramatic music and a final clip of dialogue: 'Are you frightened? Yes...Not nearly frightened enough.'

Overall, the music, voice-over and sound effects create an atmosphere of tense fear and excitement in the trailer.

A *Film poster for* Lord of the Rings

AQA Examiner's tip

When analysing media texts, try to include accurate use of media terminology.

8.6 Cross-media assignment: part 2

As part of your cross-media study, AQA GCSE Media Studies requires you to produce a research and planning assignment.

Research and plan one *print or web-based/new media task and* one *audio-visual media task.*

The print or web-based/new media task can include:

a mock-up design for a poster, magazine article, DVD case, internet home page, or other promotional material for a film.

The audio-visual task can include:

a storyboard for a trailer or a script for a television or radio interview promoting the same film.

In this assignment you will be required to:

- Devise a marketing campaign.
- Research and plan one print/web-based promotional text.
- Research and plan one audio-visual promotional text.
- Explain how your promotional material fits into your marketing campaign, and the impact it will have on your target audience.

Objectives

To look at how to approach the production task for the cross-media assignment of the controlled assessment.

Key terms

Pitch: where a writer explains and tries to sell his or her idea for a media product to a producer.

Step 1 The idea

- Discuss and produce an idea for a new film. Remember, the idea should be plausible with a potential audience. A film company will be unlikely to invest in your idea if it thinks people will not go and see the film.
- What is the genre of your film?
- Produce a **pitch** for your film. Keep this short (200 words maximum). Your pitch does not need to tell the entire story, but should sell the idea of the film.
- Come up with an appropriate title for your film.

Step 2 Research

- Make a list of the main characters in your film.
- Research and decide which actors you would choose to play your main characters. Remember to keep your choices appropriate. A-list Hollywood actors are very expensive, and are unlikely to appear in a small-budget film. Many actors specialise in certain genres or in playing certain types of role.
- Research and decide who you would choose to direct your film. You may want to find out who has directed films similar to your own.

Step 3 Planning

- Identify the target audience for your film.
- Produce a diagram to describe your target audience. Include their age, lifestyle, fashion, music tastes, etc.
- Devise a marketing strategy that will attract your target audience to your film. Think about how you might use different media, merchandise and tie-ins.

Step 4 Production

- Decide on *one* print/web-based promotional text and *one* audio-visual promotional text to produce.
- Think about how your two texts fit into your campaign. It is important that your two texts complement each other.
- Plan and produce your two texts. Remember this is a pre-production task, so if you have chosen to produce a film trailer you need to complete a storyboard sheet.

Step 5 Presentation

- For your two promotional texts, present an explanation of their potential impact on your target audience.
- In your explanation, consider where and when your promotional material would appear. Explain your choices.

A *GCSE student work: a DVD front cover*

Did you know ???????

This is how much a film studio earns for each dollar paid to a star:

Top 5:	
Vince Vaughn	$14.73
Tobey Maguire	$13.44
Julia Roberts	$13.19
Brad Pitt	$12.73
Naomi Watts	$12.16
Bottom 5:	
Jennifer Lopez	$4.10
Cameron Diaz	$4.03
Tom Cruise	$3.99
Jennifer Garner	$3.62
Nicole Kidman	$1.01

Source: Independent, *25 July 2008*

Summary

In this chapter you have looked at:

- how the film industry creates a marketing campaign
- how films are classified by their genre
- how to analyse film posters
- how to analyse film trailers
- *The Dark Knight* marketing campaign
- how to produce the cross-media assignment based on film promotion.

links

For guidance on producing storyboards, see pages 54–55.

The controlled assessment

Assignment 3. Practical production

For your third assignment for Unit 2 you have to produce an actual media product. Researching your audience, drawing up plans for your product and carrying out pre-production work are covered in Assignments 1 and 2. They will be here too, but now you have to complete the task as well.

Your teacher and/or you will choose one production task from a bank of assignments issued by AQA. This section of the book will focus on a range of these: moving image (film trailers and music videos), print (magazines) and web-based technologies/ new media. You are not allowed to repeat work from earlier assignments so, if you chose to do a film promotion campaign for Assignment 2, you can't choose to do a film trailer here for Assignment 3.

Some of the information needed for Assignment 3 will be found in other parts of this book. For instance, if you choose to produce a magazine, you will need to look at the section on analysing magazine front covers from Chapter 2 to help you in your research. When trying to identify your target audience you would be wise to refer to the pages that introduce the four key concepts, particularly the topic on audience (topic 1.2).

Before you start

Group or individual tasks?

For the practical production you are allowed to work in a group:

- of up to four people for moving image and radio/sound (film trailers, music videos, television adverts, radio shows)
- of up to two people for print- and web-based technologies/ new media (websites, magazine adverts, and magazine or newspaper pages).

If you worked in a real media environment it's almost certain that you'd be part of a team, so it makes sense to do that here. But you'll need to decide if this is right for you. Certain tasks, such as making a video, are more likely to involve group work. It's difficult to shoot film and be in shot at the same time – but not impossible! And just because someone appears in your video, it doesn't mean that they have to be in your group. You could get your mum to star in your music video, but she's not going to be getting a GCSE grade.

Some things to consider

- Do I work better on my own?
- Can I rely on the other members of the group?
- Can we pool our expertise?
- What role will we each take in a group production? (There's no point you all doing the same thing.)
- Certain tasks will expand if I work in a group. For instance, if I do the print assignment alone, I'll have to create four pages; but if I work with someone else we'll have to do four pages each.

A *The practical production can involve group work*

What type of production?

This could be decided for you. If your teacher chose to cover radio in Assignment 1 you can't do radio for Assignment 3! Your teacher may have had a very good reason for that. If your school or college doesn't have any resources or facilities for making a good audio recording then it's not wise to attempt one when 50 per cent of the controlled assessment marks are at stake. For the same reason, some schools or colleges stay clear of video, but as resources become more readily available and easier to use, there are more and more students producing lively and enjoyable moving image work that deserves high marks.

Some things to consider

- What do I enjoy and what might interest me?
- Can I produce something that would be of interest to other people (a target audience)?
- What resources do I have available?
- Can I use those resources out of school or college if I need to?
- Can anyone help me with any technical problems I might encounter?

AQA *Examiner's tip*

Whether you decide to work in a group or alone, you have to show evidence of your involvement in the project. If your group produces a stunning radio programme but your contribution was making the tea, your teacher (who will have to mark all this) won't be able to give you a very high mark.

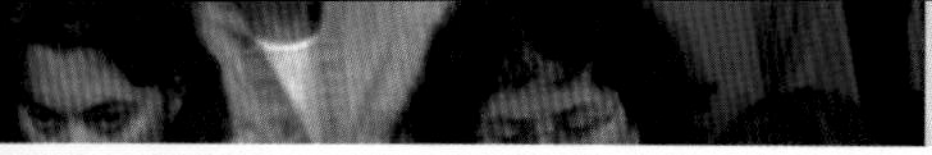

Getting started

Once you decide whether to work alone or in a group and decide what type of production you are doing, it's time to do some research.

Research

As in Assignments 1 and 2, you'll need to look at examples of existing productions in a similar genre or style to your own. If you're going to produce newspaper pages, you need to look at some real newspapers and identify the typical codes and conventions. This doesn't mean that you are going to copy the examples you look at, but you must use some aspects of the genre you're working in. There's no point making a magazine front page and not having the price on the cover. It wouldn't make your magazine original – it would make it incomplete or inappropriate. For the same reason you can't have a film trailer without any titles or a radio show that doesn't remind the listeners of the station they're tuned to.

You won't have to produce a 500-word essay on these real media texts (but you could!). You can produce an annotation or a bullet-pointed list of your findings.

Try to produce two or three pages of research referring to two or three actual media texts, which will be submitted as evidence when you hand in your work.

The next stage is to think about your audience.

Audience

One of the most important things to think about is who will consume your product. A real media text needs an audience. Who would be interested in your product? Is there a gap in the market? You might conduct market research which should provide evidence for your claims that the product is appropriate to your target audience (e.g. 'my film trailer is for a horror film that targets an audience of 15–25 year-olds. I know that this age group would be interested because…'). You could conduct surveys of your potential audience and present your research findings in the form of graphs and charts.

Try to produce two or three pages to demonstrate your audience research, which will be submitted as evidence when you hand in your work.

C *Consider audience appeal*

Putting together a brief

As a result of your research you should have a clear idea of what exactly you will be producing and what styles and techniques you will adopt. These thoughts and ideas can be written up as a brief, which is a bit like giving yourself a mission statement.

These are some ideas that may be included in a brief for a student who is part of a group that is intending to produce a newspaper:

Our newspaper will be daily/weekly/local/national… because…

The size of the paper will be… We decided on this because…

The genre or style of our newspaper is…

From our research into existing newspapers, we learned… and decided that…

Our target audience will be…

The newspaper will include… which will appeal to the target audience because…

The unique selling point (USP) of our newspaper will be…

This brief will help you to stay focused on the task at hand. You don't need to cover everything. A page or a page-and-a-half will be plenty, and you can use bullet points rather than sentences if you wish.

Planning

You don't have to do everything in rough first, but surely there'll be a planning stage! You might create sketches, bullet-pointed lists, spider diagrams, photographic contact sheets, shots from your location scouting, scripts, storyboards, mock-ups, drafts, flat plans or any other method that you think will help you to get your production moving in the right direction.

As the process continues, you will want to redraft and improve your work. To achieve the highest marks your production must look and feel like a real attempt to produce something that will interest and entertain an audience. It's the most important single piece of work for GCSE media studies – by far – so should be the result of your very best efforts.

From all your planning and redrafting material, you should submit approximately six pages of material as evidence of your planning when you hand in your work at the end of the production process.

In total, you'll submit up to 12 pages of material to demonstrate your research and planning.

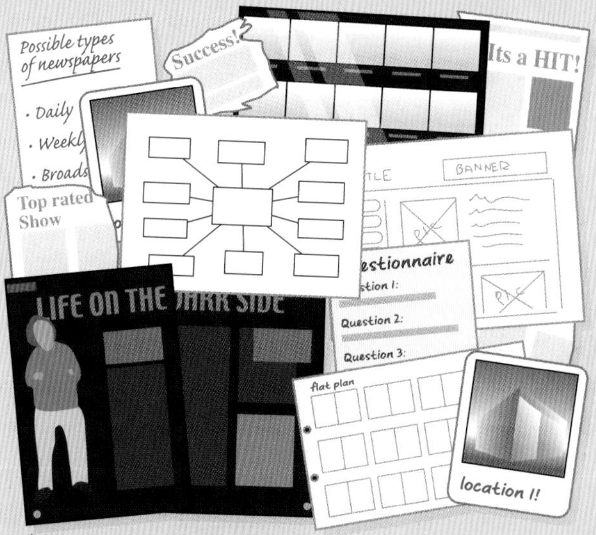

B *Perhaps you'll use some of these methods to help you with your planning*

9 Moving image

Objectives

- To look at the options available to you if you opt to create a music video.
- To look at a moving image piece and how it has been produced.

About this topic

If you select 'moving image' for your practical production you can choose to do a music video or a film trailer. If you choose 'music video', you'll need to look at Chapter 6 on music promotion. If you choose to make a film trailer, refer to Chapter 8 on film promotion.

Music video

Your research will alert you to the codes and conventions of music videos and, once you choose a song for your video, you might look at videos from the same band or artiste. Reviewing the videos of the band or artiste might be helpful but it will probably make you realise that there are lots of things that you can't do. Filming the band in concert at Wembley Stadium – not possible! Helicopter shots of the song being performed atop the Empire State Building – not possible! Morphing one face into another – not possible! So you might think that your video may not rely on performance or special effects, but with a little thought it *is* possible. The song can be performed but in a fairly intimate, low-key manner. Helicopters won't be available, but you can do an overhead shot from an upstairs window. You may not be able to 'morph', but you can dissolve and fade.

Every year students produce lively and entertaining music videos for their GCSE coursework. Some are brilliantly original and imaginative. Some use typical codes and conventions effectively to **parody** an existing video. All have to cope with fairly limited resources.

Starter activity

The stills on the next page are taken from a GCSE student's music video. Look at them carefully:

- Try to determine what genre of music this video was for.
- Write down your ideas and your reasons for making these assumptions.
- You might take a guess at the name of the artiste, or even the song.

Key terms

Parody: to imitate.

links

Refer back to the section on music videos, on pages 98–99.

A *Stills from a GCSE media studies student's music video*

9.1 Music video and genre

Codes and conventions

Objectives

To recognise how material chosen for a music video must be appropriate to the genre of the music with typical codes and conventions.

The video featured on the previous page is for a 2007 Slipknot track – *Prelude 2.0.* The genre of music could be described as rock/emo.

You might have guessed this because there are typical genre codes and conventions evident in the stills:

- The shots are not very colourful, but in black and white.
- Some of the shots are very grainy.
- There is an electric guitar.
- The 'actor' appears sad and serious.
- The mask looks scary.
- The shots in the woods are reminiscent of horror films (*Blair Witch Project*).

From the stills, it's impossible to appreciate the full effectiveness of the video and how carefully it is synchronised to the music. In many of the shots the camera is moving (panning) slowly to create an effect as if the viewer is moving, stalking the subject of the shot. The video begins slowly with shots tending to last a few seconds, but the editing speeds up (the shots change more quickly) as the song gets faster, louder and more intense.

The main difference between this and most music videos is that the song isn't performed, but the band is represented by photographs. There's a kind of performance in the use of the lyrics which appear on screen and these are synchronised with the vocals – a very tricky editing process. There may not be obvious special effects, but there is slow motion, graininess in the shots and the camera is often held at a tilted angle to convey a sense of strangeness or uncertainty.

The care, imagination and appropriateness of the video are all reasons why this achieved full marks for GCSE media studies – an A* grade.

Capturing the mood of the song

This is the work of one student using a standard video camera (worth about £200) and Windows Movie Maker to edit the film. It took several attempts to shoot the footage (probably five hours in all) and roughly 15 hours to edit. Of course, if you work successfully as a group of up to four people you can share some of the burden. With the stills on this page you have 13 images altogether from this video. Notice how different they are in terms of type of shot (long shot, close up, etc.) and also subject matter. Even so, all help to contribute to an atmosphere of menace and sadness, which is appropriate to the mood of the song. The video doesn't tell the story of the song but it does reflect the mood effectively.

A *Further stills from the GCSE media studies student's music video*

9.2 Planning your ideas

Objectives

To organise your ideas and begin planning your own video.

Getting started

Activities

Think of a song that you know well but haven't seen a video for.

1. Try to describe the genre of the song.
2. List five typical conventions of that genre.
3. List five things that you might include in a video that you could perhaps film yourself.

Example

Here is an attempt at the activity.

Song: Mardy Bum by the Arctic Monkeys

Answer

1 The genre is indie/rock.

2 Five conventions of the genre:

- a Guitars and drums
- b Casual, student dress (T-shirts, trainers, untidy hair)
- c Not smiling, but looking sly and arrogant
- d Live concerts
- e Skinny young people, males and females aged 16–25.

3 Five things to include in the video:

- a A young couple: she walks out, he looks at the camera and shrugs
- b He sings to the camera – conversational, as if he's talking to the viewer
- c 'Cuddles in the kitchen' – use the lyric, show couple laughing and hugging; medium/long shot
- d Inside of a flat, scruffy in appearance: newspapers strewn across the floor, cups left on coffee table
- e A male on a mobile phone, looking as if he's desperately trying to explain something; medium/close-up shot.

The above example attempts to follow some of the ideas of the music and lyrics – it's a fairly 'literal' interpretation of the song. But some of the best videos can appear to have very little to do with the song.

Choice of genre

Indie lends itself to making your own video because everything is meant to look fairly normal or casual. R&B might be more difficult to tackle. R&B videos are often set in glamorous locations and there is usually a great deal of sexual content – not easy to replicate in your own videos! British hip hop videos, or those for grime, or drum and bass, are more down to earth and are probably more manageable. Remember though that your video is being produced for a GCSE course, so you should really consider that a 15 certificate will be applied in terms of language, violence and so on.

Whatever genre you choose – you need to have lots of ideas!

A *Ciara in her music video for* Go Girl

B *Panic at the Disco's music video for* Nine in the Afternoon

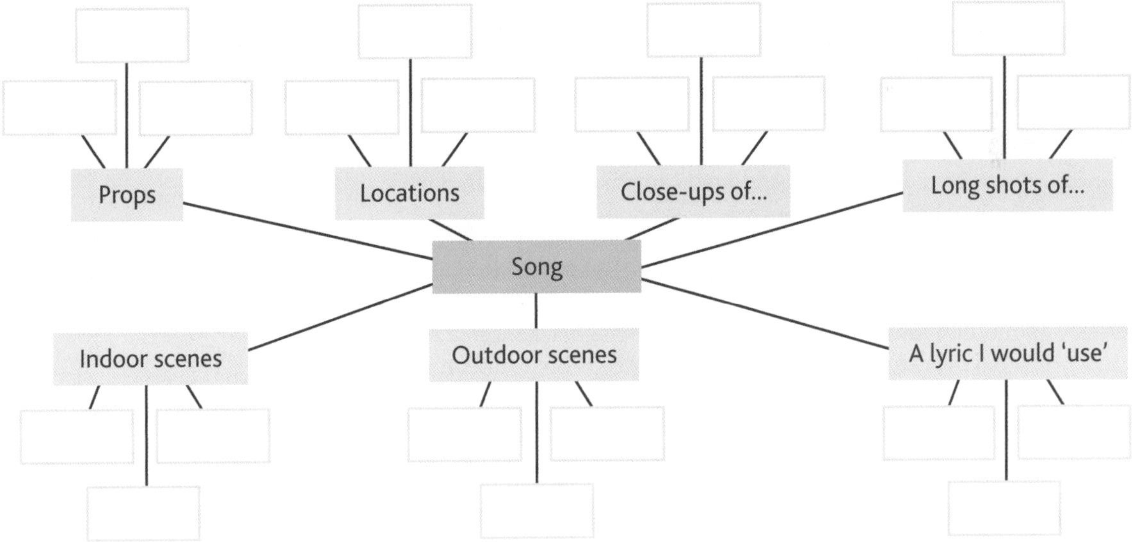

C *Spider diagrams are great for planning out your ideas*

Wastage

Be prepared to dump some of your ideas. If you only have two, that could leave you rather short! You need lots of ideas because only some of them will work. It'll be the same when you do your filming. Even with careful planning, some parts that you thought would be great could turn out to be rubbish! The more ideas you have and the more carefully you plan them, the better.

Activity

Create a spider diagram of ideas for your video.

9.3 Storyboarding

How to plan your shots

It's no good standing in a field or in the playground with a camera and trying to make things up. Each shot needs to be precisely planned. Camera movement needs to be kept to a minimum because it's difficult to keep the camera steady if you're **panning** all over the place (or **tracking**). If you can't keep the camera still or steady, your video will look amateurish. OK, so it is an amateur video, but if you use a tripod or set the camera down on a firm surface you can keep shots steady and the frame won't be wobbly! There's no visual torture worse than watching something where the camera is shaky.

You can also ensure that your video will be interesting visually by carefully planning your storyboard and making sure that you include a range of shots and techniques. Make sure that you've included long shots, close-ups, mid shots, extreme long shots and so on. Make sure that you've used some different angles. You don't want the people in the video to always be facing the camera.

If you're not very good at drawing, you can always draw up a shot list or shooting schedule instead. This just means that you will simply describe the shots you're going to use. Make sure that you consider the technical details such as shot types, camera angles, camera movement and length of shot.

Research activities

Learn from the masters!

1. Watch the D-Day landing sequence near the beginning of the movie *Saving Private Ryan*. How is the hand-held camera technique used to create a sense of urgency and danger?
2. To view a remarkable example of a tracking shot, watch the famous scene in *Mission Impossible 3* (about 102 minutes into the film), where Tom Cruise runs through the streets of Shanghai alongside a river. How did the camera operator manage to keep Tom Cruise at the centre of the shot throughout this sequence? Where was the camera?

The work of a professional

Many DVDs have extras that include storyboards, so we know that professionals rely very heavily on them. The illustrations are from Martin Asbury's storyboard from a feasibility study for a feature film. Dozens more examples of the artist's work can be found at www.martinasbury.com. Clearly this is the work of a gifted artist, but in creating our own storyboards we need to think about how we can create something visually interesting by using a variety of shot types and techniques, as Martin Asbury does here. You can also learn a great deal by simply typing 'storyboards' into a search engine.

Objectives

To learn about the importance of storyboarding and how you can create a successful storyboard.

To look at a storyboard created by a professional storyboard artist.

AQA Examiner's tip

Keep camera movement to a minimum. Panning and tracking should be seen as special effects and used sparingly to make them more effective.

Key terms

Panning: the camera is fixed at a particular point, perhaps using a tripod, but then moves from left to right (or right to left) as your eyes might as you survey a landscape.

Tracking: the camera moves with a subject, so that the subject stays in the centre of a shot. In feature films this is likely to be achieved by constructing a track on which the camera will move (a dolly track).

POV (point of view): for the second drawing in the storyboard, Martin Asbury has referred to Rachel's POV. In other words, the camera is showing what the character Rachel can see.

links

www.storyboardsoftware.com has an entertaining demo from which you can get a lot of ideas.

A *A Martin Asbury storyboard*

9.4 Editing video using Windows Movie Maker

Once you've made a fair attempt at filming your material, you'll want to start working on the editing in order to get an idea of how the finished production might look. This can prove the most time-consuming aspect of the whole exercise and, once you begin to edit, you may decide that some of your filming will need to be reshot. Still, no one said it was going to be easy! So, import your video into the computer and away you go...

Objectives

To gain an understanding of some aspects of the editing process.

Timeline or storyboard?

The Timeline view of Windows Movie Maker (see **A**) shows the components of the movie such as photos, video and audio clips in the order and timing that they will appear in the movie. It is appropriate for making music videos, because it allows you to synchronise film to a recorded track. It can also be used to add narration or backing music to a film trailer. Timeline is somewhat complicated to use, as it involves careful and precise matching of audio and video.

1 Import the audio track.

2 Drag it to audio/music timeline.

3 Split the video...

4 into shorter clips.

5 Drag these to the timeline where required.

6 Here you can add transitions and effects to the clips on the timeline.

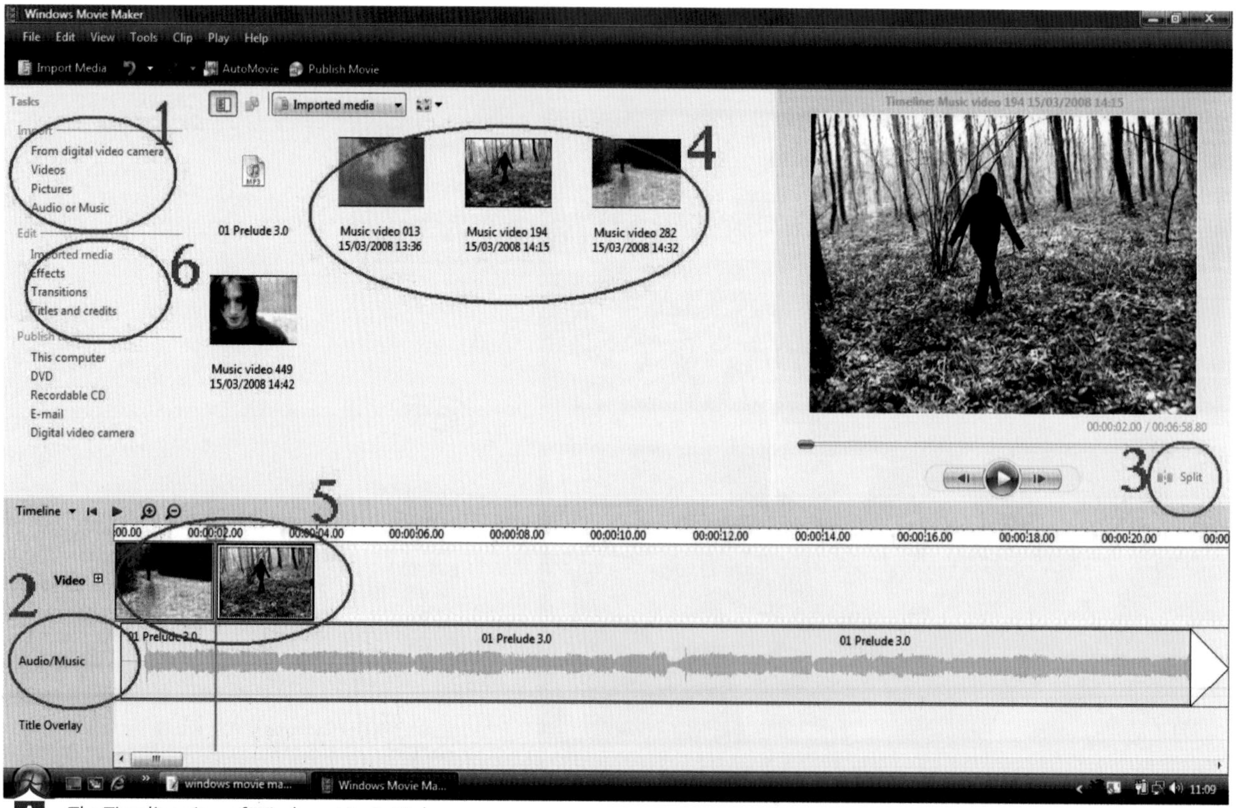

A *The Timeline view of Windows Movie Maker*

In Windows Movie Maker, the Storyboard (see **B**) is an editing area located at the bottom of the window. You create a panel of pictures or other movie clips, laid out in the sequence that they will be shown in the movie. It allows you to edit what you have filmed (which has its own audio) fairly easily. Once the film has been assembled to your satisfaction, you can switch to Timeline and add any further audio.

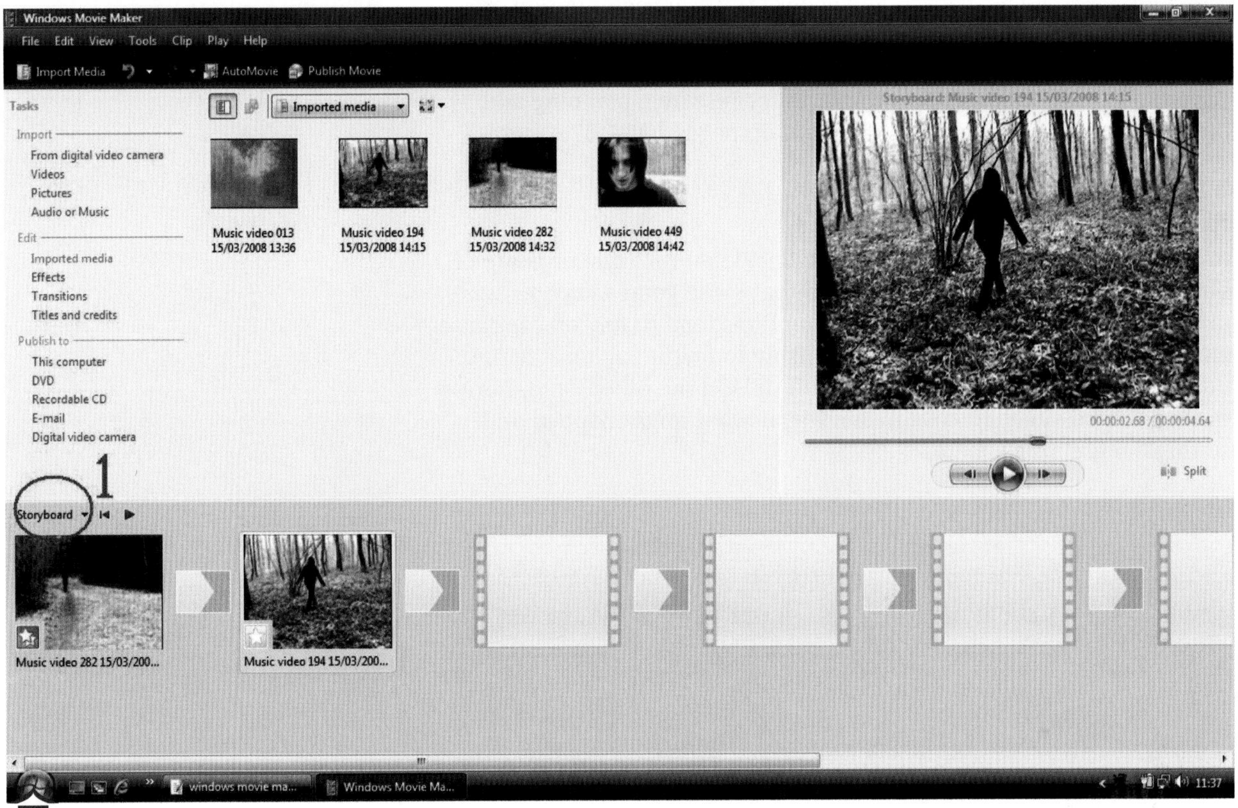

B *Windows Movie Maker Storyboard view*

Notice that there isn't a separate audio or music file alongside the images. However, the sound that has been recorded as the film has been made is incorporated into the film clips. So when you play the clips, you will hear the sound. If you wish to edit the sound, perhaps adding narration or backing music, you should switch to <u>Timeline</u> by clicking <u>Storyboard</u> (marked as 1 on **B**).

9.5 Film trailers

Most of this chapter has been concerned with the production of music video, but the other practical production moving-image option is to produce a film trailer where most of the guidance given and material offered will still be relevant. If you choose the film trailer option, you must refer back to topic 8.3 for guidance on analysing existing film trailers. This will ensure that you have a good understanding of the codes and conventions. Follow the rules for research, planning and preparation given in Unit 2 introduction on pages 134–137.

Objectives

To organise your ideas and begin planning your own film trailer.

Getting started

As with music videos, you will need to decide on the style or genre of film. Again, it's worth bearing in mind that some genres may be more difficult to approach than others. Action films tend to rely on car chases and explosions – and these would be likely to feature in a trailer. It's unlikely that you'll be able to blow stuff up! On the other hand, horror trailers can be quite effective by hinting at what might happen and setting a tense atmosphere.

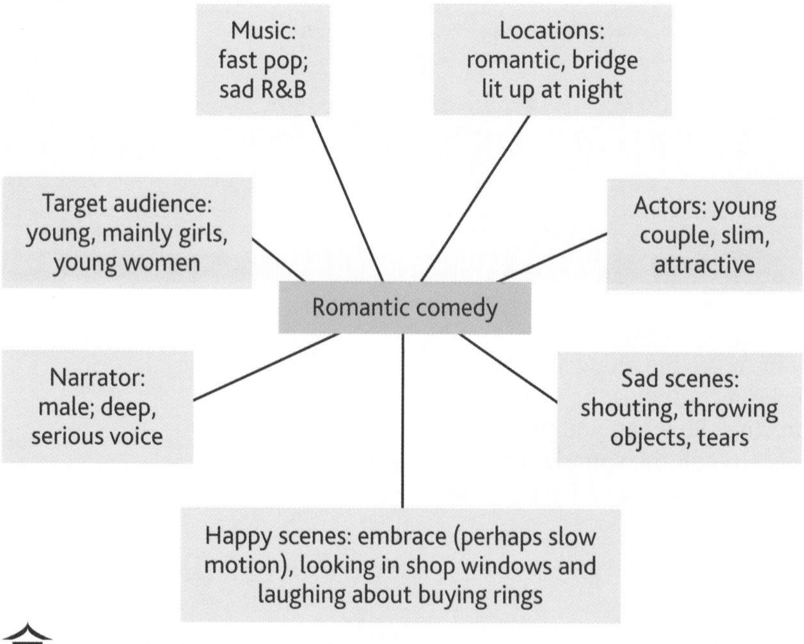

A *Use a spider diagram to consider the genre choice you might make*

The plans in diagram **A** would make for a very cheesy, very stereotypical romantic comedy! You could make it more interesting by bringing in some unusual ingredients. What if the lead actors weren't young, slim and attractive?

Activity

Produce at least one spider diagram of ideas for a film trailer in a particular genre.

What you will need to do

You will need at least 10 ideas before you can even think about the next stage.

The film trailer needs to be two minutes long. Each of your ideas might get you about 10 seconds if you edit sensibly. From your research on film trailers, you should be aware of just how many different ideas and different shots appear in an actual film trailer.

Be prepared to change and even reject ideas. There's no point wasting time on ideas that you know aren't really very good. A trailer will only give a taste of the film, so you will need to think of four or five scenes in which you will attempt to show what the actual film will be like.

Unlike music video, you have to create the idea of the film itself and are more likely to have to work with sound. In most other respects, the process is fairly similar and you'll need to follow the same steps as outlined earlier for editing music video:

- Ideastorm your ideas and produce a spider diagram, such as the one in **A**.
- Create a storyboard or shot list as you prepare to shoot your footage.
- Start shooting the footage (or filming).
- Edit your footage.

B *Plan your scenes*

C *Get a feel for your location*

9.6 Evaluating your work

The written evaluation

As part of your practical production, AQA GCSE media studies requires you to produce an evaluation.

Each candidate must produce a 700–800 word *evaluation which should reflect upon:*

how the aims of the production have been met

how the product applies appropriate codes and conventions and uses appropriate media language

how the product represents people, places or events

where and when the product would be exhibited

what regulations and controls might be applied to the product and how these have been taken into consideration

the strengths and weaknesses of the product in terms of meeting the needs of its audience.

These six statements should act as a guide. You have finished the production – how do you feel about it now?

How the aims of the production have been met

It depends on what your aims were. If you tried to make a trailer for a horror film and everyone who sees it can clearly tell that it is meant to be a horror film then you have, to a certain extent, succeeded. However, if viewers tend to laugh where you wanted them to be scared, then it may not have been a complete success! Other aims might have been: to fit the production to the required time limit, to synchronise sound and vision, to promote the song or film to its intended audience.

How the product applies appropriate codes and conventions and uses appropriate media language

Identify two or three typical genre codes and conventions or examples of effective and appropriate media language that your production displays. If you used bright colours because you did a video for a happy pop song, then that's one such example.

How the product represents people, places or events

Did you conform to stereotypes or did you challenge typical representations? What image or impression is given of the people or places featured, or the events portrayed?

Where and when the product would be exhibited

Where would people be able to see your production if it were a real media text?

Objectives

To look at how to produce the evaluation for the practical production.

What regulations and controls might be applied to the product and how these have been taken into consideration

What certificate might a film trailer be given and what restrictions on when and where it is shown might be applied to your music video?

The strengths and weaknesses of the product in terms of meeting the needs of its audience

You might need to refer back to your research and think about whether or not your production appeals to your intended audience. You may gather some feedback from people you show it to. In terms of strengths and weaknesses, you need to pick out particular details that you're pleased or disappointed with.

A *Does your production get the response you wanted from your intended audience?*

Summary

In this chapter you will have learned that for a successful practical production you need to:
research the medium or genre in which you intend to work
apply relevant codes and conventions, and media language
gather ideas by using spider diagrams or other methods
employ a range of shot types and techniques
prepare carefully using a storyboard or shot list
shoot appropriate footage and be prepared to reshoot where necessary
edit the footage carefully and precisely
evaluate the process according to the six statements from the AQA specification.

AQA Examiner's tip

With only 700–800 words, it's perfectly acceptable to present some or all of your evaluation using headings or bullet points, or any other method that avoids long description.

10 Web-based media

Assignment 3

Objectives

To learn about the different stages involved in creating a website and to start planning your own website.

An overview of the production process

What you will need to do

If your teacher or you have chosen to focus on web-based media for Assignment 3 of Unit 2, then you will have the opportunity to use your creative and technical skills to create a website aimed at a specific audience. The website should consist of four pages, including the home page.

One of the first things to consider is whether you will work individually or with a partner. Working with a partner enables you to bounce ideas off each other; you can also help each other with any technical problems you encounter. It is important to remember, however, that each of you will have to submit your own evidence of research and planning. Although you are creating one website, the requirement is to create four pages each.

The production process

In creating your website, you will work through the three stages of the production process. These are known as pre-production, production and post-production (see diagram **A**).

Pre-production

This is the planning and research part of the production process. It will involve you making important decisions about the style and content of your website and its target audience. You will need to conduct different types of audience research and investigate the style and layout of websites of a similar nature. The results of your investigations will help you to shape your product. It is at this stage that you should create designs, sketches, navigational plans and **mood boards** and try out different layouts for your proposed idea. It is far easier to work your ideas out on paper before going into full production!

Production

When you have completed all your planning and research, you will be ready to move into the production stage. This involves actually beginning to make your product, so compiling photographic and video material and writing copy for the website.

Post-production

When you have gathered all the material that you intend to use for your website (photographs, video footage and copy) you will be ready to construct the final product. This aspect of the work may involve manipulating the images that you have taken to suit

Key terms

Mood boards: used to give a sense of the style or the 'mood' of the work. They are often presented as a collection of colours, text and images that, when combined, communicate a design idea.

the purpose of the website. You might consider adding sound to the website, or perhaps you have included video which will require editing.

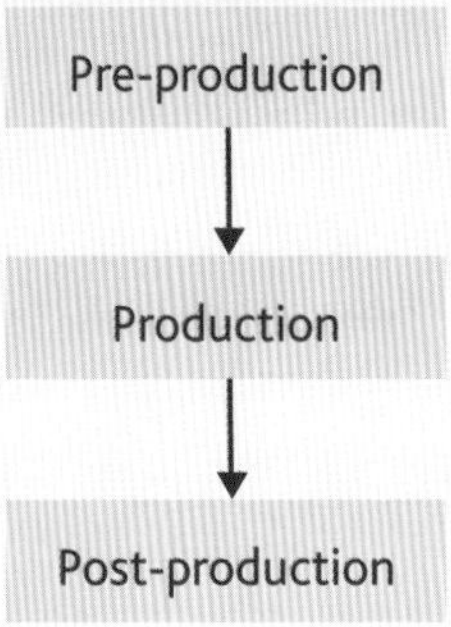

A *The relationship between pre-production, production and post-production*

To add sound or to edit video footage or animation for your website, you will need access to a range of hardware and software, for example a computer with web design software installed. A common software package is Microsoft Front Page. But if your school or college is lucky enough to have more professional software such as Adobe Dreamweaver, Flash or Photoshop, then you should consider using these packages. However, don't get carried away with the technology – it's only there to help you realise your ideas.

Evaluation

Having created your website, your final task will be to write an evaluation of between 700 and 800 words. You should try to use as much media language as possible in this work. Don't be tempted simply to describe what you did. This is an opportunity for you to analyse the production process in relation to the media theory that you have learned during your course.

Starter activity

Research a range of different websites. Is their aim to inform, educate or entertain the audience? How do they achieve this aim? What will be the main aim of your website?

10.1 Pre-production

Initial planning

The more time and effort you put into planning your project, the more likely you are to create a successful product.

Generating ideas

What will your website be about? Coming up with an idea is not always easy. In the media industry, ideas for new media products stem from a need to meet a demand from the public or the need to create a product that will generate money. Other websites are developed from an individual's desire to share information.

Whether you have decided to work on your own or with a partner, it may be useful to start brainstorming ideas for your website.

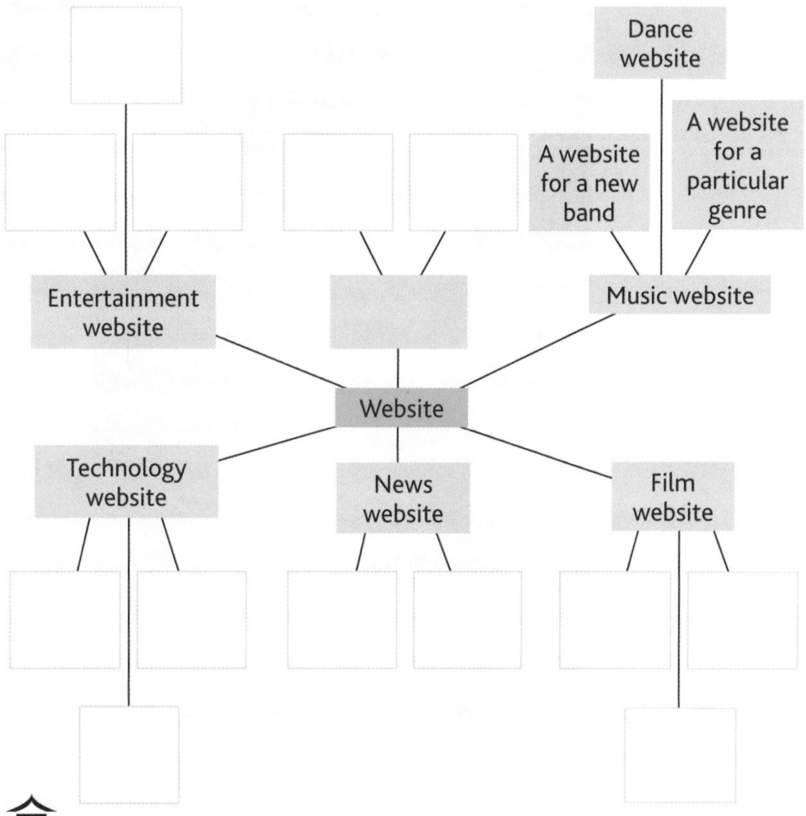

A *Start planning your ideas*

Gaining an overview of the project

Once you have an idea for a website that you wish to develop, you should attempt to get an overview of the whole project. An excellent way to do this is to apply a typical model of communication to your ideas. This communication model covers five areas. These are illustrated in diagram **B**.

Objective

To learn how to generate ideas for your website and to clearly define your target audience.

Remember

Audiences can react to media messages in different ways.

Activity

1 Copy and complete diagram **A** with ideas for different types of websites that you could create.

Choose one of your ideas to develop further. Make a list of all the content you would like to have on your website.

Extension activity

1 Research three websites that are similar in genre to the one you have chosen to create. What codes and conventions do these websites have in common?

Did you know ??????

An audience can:

Agree with the message of a text (called dominant reading).

Partly agree and partly disagree with the message of a text (called negotiated reading).

Disagree with the message of a text (called oppositional reading).

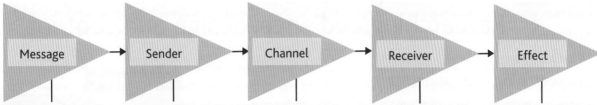

Message → **Sender** → **Channel** → **Receiver** → **Effect**

Message: What do you want to say to your audience? Can you think of one sentence which sums up the whole of your idea for a website? This will be the message.

Sender: Develop a name and logo for your company. Imagine that you work for a media company; it will encourage you to develop a professional attitude towards your work. The logo that you create could appear on your website.

Channel: There are many media channels (television, film, magazines, etc) but you have chosen the web to communicate your message.

Receiver: Describe your target audience. You will need to build a picture of your target audience so that you know how to attract them to your website.

Effect: How do you want your audience to react to your website? You may want them to contribute to a blog, to participate in a competition or to buy a product from your website. You will certainly want them to spend time looking at your website, so you will have to think of ways of engaging your audience and creating ongoing **appeal**.

B *A communication model*

Activities

2 Go online and study two different websites. What messages are they trying to communicate to their audience?

3 Describe your target audience by answering the following questions:

a How old are they?
b What is their gender?
c What is their social class?
d Where do they live?
e What jobs do they have?
f What are their hobbies and interests?
g How much do they use the internet?
h What other websites do they visit and why?

4 Design a logo for the company that you have created, using computer software such as Photoshop.

Extension activity

2 The communication model (diagram **B**) works in one direction, ending with the audience. However, many websites encourage an audience's feedback. How do websites encourage feedback and, in asking for feedback, how might the website's original message change?

Key term

Appeal: something attractive or interesting that will grab and hold your audience's attention, and make them come back to your website again.

C *GCSE student work: a logo for a website*

AQA Examiner's tip

Try to develop an overall picture of your target audience. You will find it much easier to make a product if you have a clear idea about who it is for.

10.2 Researching audience, design and content

Researching your audience

Audience research will provide information that will help you to make decisions about the design and content of your website. It will also help you to appeal directly to your audience.

Audience questionnaires

Audience questionnaires are the most convenient way of getting information. Only ask questions that you know will help you with your project. Some of your questions might relate to what the audience finds exciting about visiting websites and why they prefer the content to be delivered through this medium. You should also ask questions that relate directly to the product you are making. Give the audience information about your website and ask for their opinions. Their suggestions should contribute to your planning.

Researching design and layout

Creating mood boards

The audience research you conducted will help you to determine the design and layout of your website, but you might like to try out different ideas. Mood boards are useful to experiment with the way that the website will look. They can be created from old newspapers and magazines – any old print material – even bits of fabric! Think of the mood of your website. Is it funky or classic, or is it more gothic and dark?

The design and layout of your website is important. You want to give visual impact but don't want to compromise your message. It is a good idea to design your layout on paper first. Remember, it is far easier to change your ideas at this stage than when you have actually made the product. You will also need to consider the consistency of your design throughout the site. The conventions that you identify should be used in your own work. This will clearly establish it as part of that genre, making it easily recognisable to your audience.

Activities

1. Design a questionnaire comprising 10 questions about the website you are planning. Ask 15 people who represent your audience to complete it. Summarise the responses using graphs and charts. Consider how the information collected will influence the design of your website.
2. Use one sheet of A4 paper to create a mood board for your website. Combine images, colours and text from a variety of sources. Make sure the work reflects the mood of your website.
3. Draw a navigational plan (see diagram **C**), which shows the four pages of your website and how users will get around the website.

Objectives

- To learn about ways of researching your audience.
- To begin to develop the design and layout of your website and investigate ways to generate content.

links

Look at the section on web analysis (pages 78–79) for more information on consistency of design and branding.

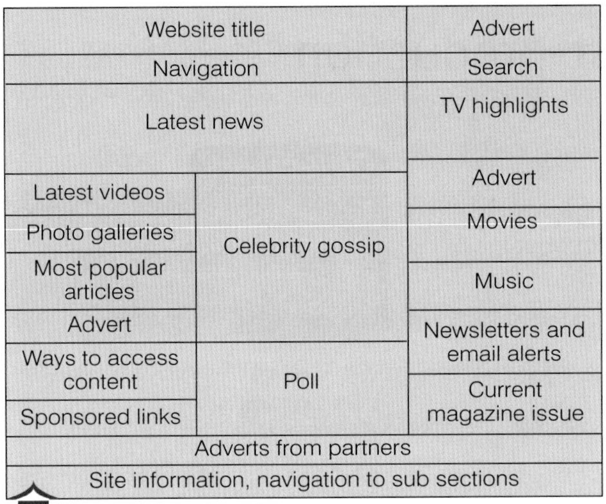

A *A rough plan of a web page*

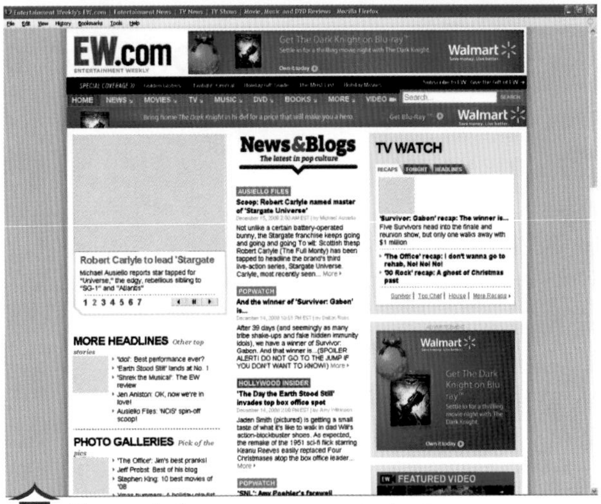

B *The rough plan converts to an actual web page*

Navigational plan

You have to create four pages for your website and one must be the home page. This page will probably contain lots of information. However, be aware that too much information will simply be off-putting to the user who may not know where to look first. One of the most important elements of your home page will be the navigational links – but where will these links lead? Creating a navigational plan will solve the problem and help to you see how all four pages of your website connect together and, more importantly, how the audience will be able to navigate around your website.

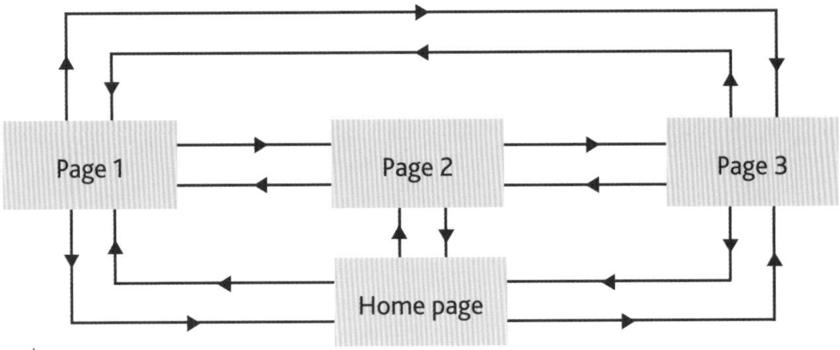

C *Navigational plan*

Extension activity

Choose one entertainment website and draw a navigational plan, as in diagram **C**, that reflects the sites construction.

Researching content

Your website will need content, which should be, as far as possible, original. This gives you the opportunity to be creative. You should plan the copy for your website as well as the photographs and any video that you want to use. You may want to interview people to include articles on your website. Researching the content of your website might take some time and you might have to involve other people. You should have a **contingency plan** in case things don't go as anticipated! What would you do if the person you have arranged to attend a photo shoot on a specific date and at a specific time fails to turn up?

Key terms

Contingency plan: a plan that can be put in place for an event or circumstance that is possible but might not happen.

10.3 Production and post-production

Production

Once you have completed the planning and research (the pre-production stage), you will need to produce the content for your website. Your website will include some or all of the following:

- photography
- video
- copy
- advertising
- sound and animation.

The content should be your own work. Creating your own photographs and copy is far more difficult than downloading material from the internet, but it is more rewarding and it shows your creative skills. Even the adverts could be ones that you have designed yourself!

Objectives

To learn how to produce the content for your website and to edit the material into a finished product.

Activity

How will you represent the people, objects or places that appear in your website? What 'image' are you trying to create?

A *Manipulation of original imagery – before*

B *Manipulation of original imagery – after*

When generating the content for your website, you are involved in a process of representation. Look at the student work in **C**. A Year 11 student, has constructed his music website using elements that are representative of hip hop culture. The student's audience recognises the link to hip hop because he has used a visual language that is familiar to them. The style, colour and size of the text are appropriate for the genre of the website he is creating.

C *GCSE student work: a home page representative of hip hop*

Post-production

Once all of the production activities have taken place, you will be ready to start assembling the final product. This involves turning the initial designs into reality. You will combine photographs, video and copy based on the design you initially created. You may need still image and moving image software to edit the raw material and, of course, you will need web authoring software to combine the various elements.

Your school or college may have a range of this software in varying degrees of complexity. Don't think you need to use top-level software to get a top-level product, however. Professional software is impressive, but it is possible to achieve as high a grade for your work having used Microsoft's FrontPage, as it is if you had used Adobe Dreamweaver. The technology should simply support your creative ideas. Perhaps your school or college has one or more of the following software packages:

- Microsoft Front Page
- Adobe Dreamweaver
- Adobe Flash
- Adobe Photoshop
- Adobe Premiere
- Windows Movie Maker or iMovie (MAC)
- Final Cut Pro.

All of this software does require a level of skill. If you need to learn how to use it, you will have to factor this in to the time you have to complete the project.

Once you have completed the work, you will need to export it and test that all the links work. You may need to make adjustments at this stage to ensure that the user experience is satisfying. If you can, test your website in a web browser.

You will also want to test your work on your audience. Their reactions will be crucial and could give you the opportunity to make changes before going 'live'.

Extension activity

What on your website will signify that it targets the audience you have chosen? How will this content engage the interest of that audience? What changes would you make to target a different audience?

Remember

You might need to use specialist equipment owned by your school or college to construct your website. Some of your friends might want to use the same equipment at the same time as you. Do you need to book out equipment in advance?

Did you know ??????

You can usually download a free trial of the software listed above from the respective websites. Do a search online and see what you can find. It may be easier, however, to install the software at home rather than at school.

There are many books available which cover the technical aspects of web design. Ask your teacher for recommendations.

AQA Examiner's tip

It is helpful to keep a diary of your progress. This will be useful when you come to evaluate the product.

links

Refer back to pages 78–79 on website analysis.

Pages 76–77 on web-based media gives details of the conventions that you might incorporate in your website.

10.4 Evaluating your work

The written evaluation

You now need to write an evaluation of between 700 and 800 words. This evaluation should reflect upon the following.

How the aims of the production have been met

You started this project with a message that you wanted to send to your audience via the internet. How successful were you in achieving this aim? Did you work to the plan that you set out at the beginning of the project and/or did you have to make modifications as you went along?

How the product applies appropriate codes and conventions and uses appropriate media language

In what ways have you used the codes and conventions related to your chosen genre to inform the construction of your website? Your visual style, including general layout, colours and text should be consistent across the site and will contribute to your particular **house style**.

How the product represents people, places and events

Your website will have content on it. This may have been presented through text, moving and still images. You have made decisions about how this content is to be presented to the audience. What type of representations have you constructed in your work and how might these be read by your audience?

How people will be able to see your website

Simply uploading your website does not guarantee that it will be seen! Some may stumble across your website whilst browsing the internet. Others may do a search and find your website a result. Have you considered ways in which your audience might get to see the website? One popular way of getting exposure is to have a link on another site which, when clicked, takes the user to your website. Depending on the type of website, you may have to consider promoting it in other mediums. In any case, you need to try and get maximum exposure for your website.

What regulations and controls might be applied to the product and how these have been taken into consideration

There are many laws covering the activities of the media in this country. In addition there are a number of regulatory bodies whose purpose it is to monitor the output of various media platforms. Self-regulation of the media seems to be the preferred method because it allows greater freedom. The internet, however, is fairly unregulated compared with other media platforms Of course, any content on the internet is subject to the general laws of the land but, in practice, this has been difficult to enforce. Much of the regulation therefore has come down to **Internet Service Providers (ISP)** who have the ability to remove individual websites.

Objectives

To be able to evaluate your work in relation to the production process and your knowledge of the four key concepts.

Activities

1. Describe all the conventions that you have used in your website. In what ways do these reflect the expectations of your target audience? What is your particular house style?
2. Why do you think the internet is difficult to regulate? How has your website been regulated? It may be that your school has a set of rules that you have to observe. This is a form of regulation.

links

Look at the section on website analysis, which begins on pages 76–77, to learn some of the media language associated with web-based media.

Key terms

House style: the identity of a media product which makes it easily recognisable to its audience.

links

Read the section on uses and gratifications on pages 12–13.

The strengths and weaknesses of the product in terms of meeting the needs of its audience

It is useful to conduct some audience feedback research. Compiling an audience questionnaire is one way to do this. Remember, you are trying to ascertain how successful the work has been and how far it has met the needs of the audience, so your questions should reflect this. You could also arrange a user group to test out the website and to feed back their comments to you face to face. If you can include people outside your peer group then even better – though be prepared for some responses that you didn't expect!

You may have kept a diary or log of your work as it progressed. This will be very useful for writing your evaluation.

A *Why did you do what you did? How did you do it?*

AQA Examiner's tip

Don't spend too much time describing the process you went through. Concentrate on the 'how' and 'why' rather than the 'what'. Make sure you continue to use appropriate media terms in your analysis.

Remember

Even if you have worked in a group, you will need to write your own evaluation.

AQA Examiner's tip

Researching your audience will be a very important aspect of your pre-production work. The more you know about your intended audience, the more likely you are to create a product that meets their needs and interests.

kerboodle!

11 Producing a magazine

Assignment 3

Objectives

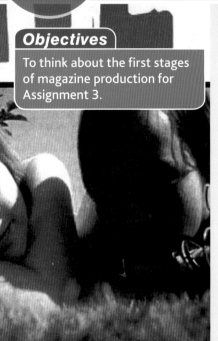

To think about the first stages of magazine production for Assignment 3.

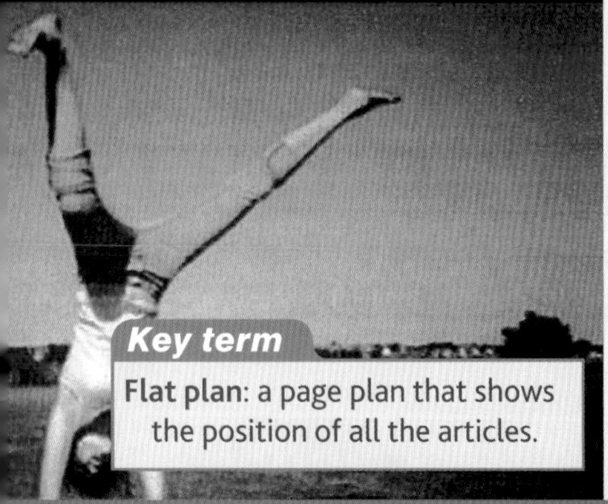

Key term

Flat plan: a page plan that shows the position of all the articles.

Planning and research

What you will need to do

If you or your teacher has chosen to focus on print for Assignment 3 of Unit 2, then you will have the opportunity to put your creative skills and knowledge of magazines to good use, to create some pages of your very own magazine:

- You can work individually or with one other person.
- If you work alone, you need to produce four pages of a magazine, including the front cover.
- If you work with a partner, you need to produce four pages each (a total of eight pages).
- You need to produce an evaluation of your work that is between 700 and 800 words.

Guidance

Here are some points to consider if you are thinking of producing a magazine:

- Do you have access to a computer? What software package will you use? (There is a wide variety of sophisticated desktop publishing (DTP) software available, although effective magazine work can be produced using basic DTP software such as MS Publisher.)
- What will your magazine be about? Is it a general-interest magazine or a specialist magazine?
- Who is your intended target audience?
- When deciding on your type of magazine, try not to choose something too obvious. You will gain extra marks if you can produce a magazine where you are not the intended target audience.
- Wherever you can, try to use original material. This includes writing your own articles and organising your own photography.
- If you need to use existing material, such as images from the web, try to manipulate them for your magazine, so that you can still demonstrate creativity.
- Remember, you only need to produce *four pages* (if working individually), so aim to make all of your pages look as professional as possible.
- If you are going to work as part of a pair, make sure you choose someone whom you trust to help make your production a success.

- Do not forget the planning stage and the evaluation. These are just as important as producing the actual magazine.

Pre-production

Research

As part of the pre-production of your magazine assignment, you need to carry out some research:

- Study other similar magazines. Look carefully at their design.
- While you may wish to include some aspects of the competition in your production, what will be distinctive about your magazine?
- Is there a gap in the market for your magazine? You could carry out a survey of your target audience. What does the survey tell you?
- In what ways is your magazine going to be different from other, similar magazines?
- What are the codes and conventions of these magazines?
- Examine the adverts that appear in these magazines.

Planning

Before you actually produce your magazine, it is important to carry out a certain amount of planning. Remember you will be marked on your planning and research. Planning could include:

- a **flat plan** of your pages
- sketches, mock-ups and drafts of your pages, including the front cover
- masthead design
- page design and layout
- photographs.

Your planning should demonstrate how your production has evolved, so try to annotate your work, and explain your design ideas. If you have changed some of your design ideas, include your original drafts, and explain why you have changed them.

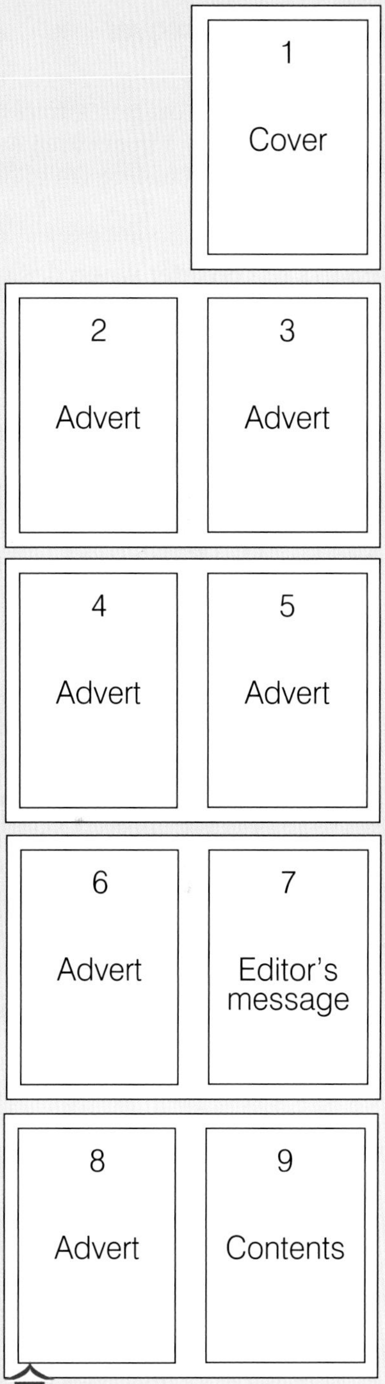

A *A flat plan for the opening pages of a women's glossy*

11.1 Producing the magazine

The front cover

The front cover is the most important page of a magazine. Titles depend on their covers to attract readers, so a great deal of effort is put into the design of a front cover. As part of your research you need to look at the layout and design of front covers and consider what makes an effective cover.

Points to consider when designing a front cover

- Is it clear from the cover what the magazine is about?
- Will your front cover appeal to your target audience?
- Does your cover include the appropriate conventions?
- Does your cover have visual impact?
- Do the masthead and cover lines stand out?

The contents page

The contents page is significant because, unlike any other page, it shows the structure of a magazine. These pages usually contain a list of features and articles and their respective page numbers. Sometimes they also include descriptions of the articles, and institutional information about the magazine. Contents pages often contain sample images from articles in the magazine.

As part of your research, you need to look at examples of contents pages and identify the conventions of these pages. Sometimes student magazines concentrate on the design of front covers, with less attention given to the contents page. However, as with the front cover, a contents page needs careful planning and design.

Points to consider when designing a contents page

- Does your contents page include the appropriate conventions?
- Does your contents page make the articles appear exciting and interesting to read?
- Would the articles and features that you have indexed appeal to your target audience?
- Does your contents page index the features referred to from the front page cover lines?
- How have you organised your contents? Are there special features and regular features?
- How have you used fonts and colour to make your contents page appealing?
- Have you managed to include original photography?

Objectives

To look at the design and layout of magazine front covers and contents pages.

links

For more information on magazine front covers, see pages 22–26.

Remember

Your contents page needs to make reference to articles from the complete magazine. Even though you may only be producing a small sample of pages, thought is needed when referring to other features and articles that would appear in your magazine.

Contents

Issue 306 Summer 2008

For breaking gear news, visit musicradar.com

News Reviews Tuition Samples Forums Community

80
Dream semi shoot-out
By popular reader demand, we put three single-cut semi-hollowbody guitars from Carvin, PRS and Collings through their paces in this revealing comparative review

Every issue...

3 Welcome... The editor speaks
10 Feedback Reader's lives
14 Frontend Guitar news and views
28 Perfect 10 Myles Kennedy of Alter Bridge
31 Column Guitar Geek Charles Shaar Murray
32 Column Rock Climbing Jon Stewart
34 Fretbuzz Upcoming bands: Martin Harley, Johnny Winter, Matt Anderson, Exit Ten. PLUS video lessons on the CD
140 Subscribe Pay less, get a gift. No brainer?
145 Tips Q&A Your gear queries answered
150 Used Gear How to buy a VOX Mk VI 1965
152 Coming Next Month/ USA Subscriptions
157 Music Reviews Guitar DVDs and CDs
184 Reader Ads Buy, sell, exchange and recruit
194 CD contents Find out what's on your CD

Summer 2008 Guitarist 7

Contents

This Month

42 John Mayer
This Stateside megastar's profile is rising fast in the UK. Amazing blues-based playing, slick songwriting and a signature Strat to boot – Guitarist meets him to find out more...

58 Sonny Landreth
We ask Landreth about the making of his star-studded new album, From The Reach

52 Ry Cooder
The slide master rarely gives interviews, but Guitarist caught up with him on the completion of his recent Californian trilogy of albums

64 Steven Van Zandt
E-Street mainstay, solo artist, UN peace ambassador and Sopranos star Steven Van Zandt gives us the lowdown on playing dirty

88 Fender Billy Corgan Signature Strat
Tribute for Smashing Pumpkins guitarist

106 Martin OM Davy Graham
Martin honours the great folk guitarist

110 Orange OR50H
Orange revives the spirit of 1972 with its new single-channel head

TERMS AND CONDITIONS

Gear Reviews

80 Carvin SH575, Collings SoCo & PRS Hollowbody Singlecut An exclusive, three-way single-cut semi-hollowbody shoot-out
88 Fender Billy Corgan Stratocaster A smashing new signature model
94 Duesenberg D-Caster & D-Bass 5 Two great new additions to the quirky-cool German brand
100 Parkwood PWH4 Hybrid Electric and acoustic, all in one
102 Huss & Dalton FS & DS-12 A pair of wallet-busting yet very tempting acoustics
106 Martin OM Davy Graham The new signature model from a legend of British folk
110 Orange OR50H head A fruity pipsqueak to help celebrate 40 years of great British amps
115 Emerson Williams Bluestone Pro Load Box Amp too loud? You need one of these
118 BOSS GT-10 The best GT floor-based processor yet? Find out here
122 DigiTech RP500 Good value and great tones
126 Carl Martin Echotone The perfect fix for your inner delay junkie
128 Vigier Excess II Roger Glover Original bass Smoke and water not included
132 Native Instruments Guitar Rig Session The last excuse to ignore computer-based recording has gone
136 Quick Test Flightcase Spider SPC450 pedal case, ProGuard Customised Earplugs, Sweetsound Mojo Vibe, Crate Profiler Model 5
142 Longterm Tests Blackstar Artisan 30, PRS Mira, Epiphone Les Paul Ultra II

Guitarist CD
See page 194

8 Guitarist Summer 2008

A *The contents page of* Guitarist *magazine comprises a double-page spread*

Contents
November 2008

8 **Your letters** A Pavlovan response to waste
11 **Flavours of the month** Grow, cook, eat...

Appetisers
15 **Word of mouth** Get the taste for loose tea
16 **This month we love...** A fig-coloured tagine
18 **Books of the month** Gastropubs and grits
20 **VIP** Stefano Cossi is a bright young brewer
22 **Signature dish** Julian Fellowes explains his *vitello tonnato* (without the veal)
24 **Ten ways with...** Celeriac
26 **Tasting notes** A selection of olives

Features
30 **Homemade** Tropical Christmas cake
35 **My recipe inheritance** Sally Clarke shares her late father's Turkish delight
36 **Steen grills...** Giorgio Locatelli reveals the agony and heartbreak behind his cooking
46 Cover story **Just give in!** An absurdly tempting chocolate fondant pudding
49 Cover story **The most useful kitchen gadgets of all time (and the most useless)** What's the greatest culinary tool?
56 Cover story **Game ideas for duck, venison and partridge** Anthony Demetre, our guest chef, takes the pain out of game
70 **Portraits** A gallery of real-life Willy Wonkas
81 Cover story **Delia's amazing 40-minute roast pork** The Save Our Bacon campaign receives a litter of piggy dishes from five pork experts, including Mrs Smith
88 **Travel** Katy Salter tries to live the Heidi dream at the St Moritz Gourmet Festival
93 **Cocktails** Sundowners and canapés at the St Moritz hotel in Cornwall
103 **Kev in the community** Kevin Gould meets the Portuguese residents of Thetford
107 **Drinking** The *WFI* team pick their party favourites and Andrew Jefford compares different strength wines. Plus, fruit beers
112 **Eating out** Sitwell scoffs at The Connaught. Plus, country house hotels around the UK, new openings and dining on chocolate.
122 **A question of taste** Julie Walters

Biting Talk
32 William Sitwell wishes a very happy 21st birthday to Bibendum
42 Liz Marcy says 'no thanks' to Thanksgiving
77 A new wave of restaurateurs is keeping chefs in their place, says Bill Knott. Plus, Stephen Bayley on cocktails
100 Mrs Santini's advice on exes and eggs

Offers & competitions
28 **Join...** Delia's food and wine workshop
28 **Subscribe...** and get a Brabantia slide bin
34 **Win...** seven nights in a Thai paradise
117 **Visit...** Taste of Christmas in London

56 **Marinated venison steaks are a great way to enjoy game**

88 **The Swiss Alps host Europe's finest chefs for a festival of food**

93 **A pear bellini tastes even better in the Cornish twilight**

WAITROSE FOOD ILLUSTRATED 5

B *The images of this contents page from* Waitrose Food Illustrated *have been selected to tie in with a winter edition*

11.2 Producing a spread

Creating a spread involves more than filling a page with text and a few pictures. As with your previous pages, you will need to research and plan your spreads.

Research

Have a close look at a variety of magazine spreads:

- How are the spreads designed?
- Where do you find your attention drawn to on a page?
- How is the content and style of the magazine reflected in the layout?
- How are columns used in the spread?
- What styles of text are used? Have different fonts been used?
- What do you notice about the size and layout of the images?
- How have captions been used with the images?

Planning your text

- What type and size of font will you use? A common mistake is to choose a large font size. Magazines often use a small font size for the main text. However, if your magazine is for young children, a large font is appropriate.
- You may wish to use different fonts for separate sections, such as a side panel. However, you shouldn't need more than three different fonts for your text. Too many fonts will create a confused style.
- All magazines have a 'house style'. This is a consistent set of standards for design and writing a document. You need to create a 'house style', so that all your pages look like they belong together.

Entry points

A magazine is not a book, and readers rarely read a magazine from cover to cover. Instead a magazine is designed to be a casual read. It is glossy, highly visual and designed to be dipped into. Therefore single- and double-page spreads need careful design so that they can hook the reader as they are flicking through the magazine. There are a variety of techniques for doing this and they are known collectively as **entry points**.

The example pages in **A** shows a typical double-page spread, and highlights key entry points.

Did you know ???????

Our attention is naturally drawn to the top right-hand corner of double-page spreads. Advertisers will often seek to place their adverts in this position, as it is the 'facing page'. A strong image will have more impact in this position.

Objectives

To learn about the layout and design of text in magazine spreads.

Key terms

Entry point: small bits of information or visual interest designed to catch the eye and give a quick fix of content that leaves the reader wanting more.

Panel
Also known as a 'boxout', this contains separate info which may or may not be related to the page's main text.

Slug
Included on most pages, this tells the reader where they are. A coloured bar or tab is often used to add impact to the page.

Subhead
This clarifies or contextualises the headline. When placed above (as here) rather than below, it's sometimes called a 'superhead'.

Standfirst
This is a 'teaser' for the story, summarising its theme to get the reader interested, without giving away key points or conclusions.

WOB
White text on a coloured background is said to be 'reversed out', and the technique is traditionally referred to as 'WOB' (white on black).

Wild! DIARY

Not to be missed...

Wednesday 11 July
AT HOME WITH THE TERRAPINS
23 Acacia Avenue, Miltham
7.30pm for 8pm
Richard and Judy Spottiswoode will be hosting a cheese and wine party for reptile lovers. Please bring your own – cheese and wine that is, not reptiles! (Though Richard promises there will be an opportunity for that later in the summer, when the gazebo is finished.)

Tuesday 17 July
HEADS UP, IT'S THE MEERKATS!
Community Hall,
Keith Chegwin Retirement Complex
3pm sharp
Donald Magee presents video highlights of his trips over the past 15 years to investigate the mating behaviour of the enchanting rodents made famous by a BBC documentary. (Not suitable for epilepsy sufferers.)

Friday 20 July
WILDLIFE ACTION NW AGM
Pizza Hut, Lower Wedging
7pm
A must for all members who want a say in next year's activities, or to seek election to the Committee. Our guest speaker this year is Mrs Eve Borage, former PA to Tony Soper.

10 JULY 2001

■ **LOCATION REPORT**

Stars and stripes

STEVE McNAMARA talks to two Wildlife Action NW members about their trip of a lifetime to see South Africa's zebras

WHEN BOB AND SUE UNDERWOOD RETURNED TO SOUTH Africa last year after more than two decades away from their former home country, revisiting old friends was second on their list of priorities. Their prime motivation was to make the acquaintance of a group they'd never had the time to get to know: the local zebra population. We all know this animal from pre-school picture books, of course, but the zebra is a source of great fascination to zoologists and lay admirers alike, and is certainly more than just a 'horse of a different colour'.

"The chief enemies of the zebra are lions and hunters, who kill them for their flesh and hide."

Native to Africa, the zebra is smaller in size than the related horse and greatly resembles the wild ass in habit and form, having a short, erect mane, large ears, and a tufted tail. The stripes, which distinguish this animal from other members of the horse family, serve as protective coloration in its natural habitat. The chief enemies of the zebra are lions and hunters who kill zebras for their flesh and hide. Zebras can be trained to work in harness and are popular animals in zoos and circuses. Three species and several subspecies are generally recognized, chiefly according to variations in the arrangement of the stripes.

The mountain zebra is the smallest species, averaging about 1.2 m (about 4 ft) high at the shoulders, and has a strong, muscular, and symmetrical body. It is silver-white, striped with black markings that extend to every part of the body except the stomach and the inner part of the thighs. The markings on the head are brown, and the muzzle is a rich bay-tan. The legs are short and wiry.

Mountain zebras travel in small herds and inhabit the mountain ranges of South Africa. This species was formerly plentiful but has been decimated by intensive hunting. Burchell's zebras travel in large herds and inhabit the central and eastern plains; the species is named after the British naturalist William John Burchell. They are pale yellow with broad, black stripes, generally interspersed with fainter markings which are known as shadow stripes.

Variations on a theme
The species has several variations, some have stripes down to the hooves, and the lower legs of others are solid white without any stripes. The Boers refer to all varieties of Burchell's zebra as quaggas. The true quaggas, however, were exterminated during the 19th century, they were darker in color than the zebra and striped only on the head, neck, and shoulders. The largest species, Grévy's zebra, is named after the former French president Jules Grévy. It attains a height of about 1.5 m (about 5 ft) at the shoulders, and its stripes ▶

ZEBRAS Wild!

Horse of a different colour: there's more to the zebra than first meets the eye

NOW YOU SEE ME...
Contrary to popular belief, the zebra's distinctive pattern does not camouflage it as such. Rather, the stripes break up the outline of each animal in a group, thus confusing any predator trying to identify a target.

JULY 2001 11

Byline
Publising speak for the writer's name. It usually goes either in the standfirst, often in bold or caps, or at the story's end in italics.

Drop cap
A dropped capital, or drop cap, is an age-old way of helping the reader out by drawing attention to the start of an article.

Pullquote
A pull-out quote or pullquote magnifies a particularly interesting or controversial sentence to draw the reader into the text.

Sidebar
Despite its name, it doesn't have to be on the side, but this smaller block of text offers a handy nugget of info or an entertaining aside.

Crosshead
These small , often meaningless headings help break up the text and make the page look less daunting to read.

Folio
Another slug appears at the bottom outside edge, showing the page number (folio), title and/ or date.

A *A typical double-page spread with the text features highlighted*

11.3 Evaluating your work

The written evaluation

As part of your practical production, AQA GCSE Media Studies requires you to produce an evaluation.

Each candidate must produce a 700–800 word *evaluation which should reflect upon:*

how the aims of the production have been met

how the product applies appropriate codes and conventions and uses appropriate media language

how the product represents people, places or events

where and when the product would be exhibited

what regulations and controls might be applied to the product and how these have been taken into consideration

the strengths and weaknesses of the product in terms of meeting the needs of its audience.

How the aims of the production have been met

Now that you have finished your magazine, has it turned out the way you originally planned?

Some key questions might include:

- **How organised were you (and your partner)**? Did you complete the production on time? If you worked with another student, did you work well as a team?
- **How effective is your magazine production**? Does the front cover grab your attention? Are your spreads exciting and interesting to read? Does it look professional?
- **Did you keep to your original plans or did you have to modify your production**? If you made changes, explain how and why your production changed.

How the product applies appropriate codes and conventions and uses appropriate media language

How effective is the layout and design of your front cover, contents page and spreads? In your answer make reference to your research of magazine design. Also try to include the correct terminology. For example, how effective is your use of **pull quotes** and **drop caps**? How effective has been your use of images and photography? Is there a **house style** to your production? If so, how have you achieved this?

Objectives

To look at how to produce the evaluation for the practical production.

Key terms

Pull quotes: quotations from an article that are placed in a larger font, on the same page, to entice the reader into the story.

Drop cap: the first letter of a paragraph that is enlarged to 'drop' down two or more lines.

How the product represents people, places or events

What impression does your magazine give about the people and places featured? Think about how you have portrayed people. Did you conform to stereotypes or did you challenge typical representations? If you were aiming to attract both genders, how have you achieved this? Have you portrayed your target audience within the magazine? If so, explain your representation.

Where and when the product would be exhibited

If your magazine was a real media product, where would people be able to see or buy it? Think about where, when and how your target audience might buy or read your magazine. Also include how often it would be published: weekly or monthly? If your magazine has a cost, how much would you charge and why?

What regulations and controls might be applied to the product and how have these been taken into consideration?

If your magazine was a real media product, what restrictions would there be about what you could and could not publish?

The strengths and weaknesses of the product in terms of meeting the needs of its audience

How effectively does your production appeal to its intended audience? An excellent way to respond to this question is to try your magazine out on your target audience. What do they think about your production? What do they think are strengths and weaknesses of the production? You may wish to include quotations or a summary from a questionnaire. Think about the needs of your audience. Have you met these in your magazine?

A *Keep your audience in mind*

AQA Examiner's tip

In your evaluation:

- Use headings and bullet points.
- Be honest and critical.
- Do not write lengthy descriptions of your production.
- Do not go over the 700–800 word limit.

Remember

If you have worked in a pair, you will need to write your own evaluation.

links

Read the section on uses and gratifications on pages 12–13.

11.4 Examples of students' magazine productions

BRITAINS NO.1 MUSIC MAGAZINE OF THE YEAR!
ONLY £1.60!
ISSUE NUMBER 103
Sept/Oct
MOOSIK
www.moosik.co.uk
INTERVIEWS
with
THE LENGTHS
WITTY PINK
BROKEN #15
WICKED CHICKENS
PLUS!
ALBUM REVIEWS
TOUR DIARY OF
THE BUFFALOS!
+ MUCH MORE!
THE TWINS
DOUBLE THE FUN AS THEY FL IN TO
2008 WITH THEIR BRAND NEW ALBUM!
ANCY YOUR CHANCES OF WINNING TICKETS TO DOWNLOAD FEST FOR 2008?

A *Front cover*

- An effective colour scheme has been created by selecting a limited number of colours that combine well.
- Alternating colours and graphic features draw attention to the cover lines.
- Banners highlight the logo and competition feature.
- A creative masthead helps establish the magazine's identity.
- Original photography has been successfully used for the cover photograph.

Objectives

To look at an example of work produced by some GCSE media studies students.

Key terms

Slug: a short heading indicating the subject of the copy.

A lively and exciting contents page:

- Notice how the students have continued the colour scheme that was used on the front cover.
- Again, highly effective use of original photography attracts the reader to the articles.
- Notice how the list of contents is divided, and how further detail is given with the page headings.
- The students have produced an engaging and dynamic spread.
- Digital effects have been used to create interest and variety in the photographs.
- Creative text helps to reinforce the identity of the band.
- Entry points, such as the pull quote and headings, draw in the reader.
- Look at the text. Thoughtful selections of colour, font and size create an interesting and attractive spread.
- The use of a drop cap draws in the reader.
- The **slug** shows the page number and title.

P18
THE TWINS
This month in...
MOOSIK
ISSUE 103
We hunted them down for the latest diaries on their UK tour.
THE P4
BUFFALOS
We find out what The Twins have been up to and what we can expect from them in the New Year
P32
THE
LENGTHS
We have a lengthy interview with new band, The Lengths
The two-piece band have announced that they are set to lay out a list of tour dates by next easter.
P24
WICKED
CHICKENS

CONTENTS

REGULARS

P10 TOP 10 ALBUMS
P12 TOP 10 SINGLES
P14 COMPETITIONS
P20 LIVE GIG REVIEWS
P22 PODCASTS
P28 HOT STUFF
P36 FREE! GUITAR CHORDS
P40 MYSPACE REVIEWS
P44 SERVICES DIRECTORY

SPECIAL FEATURES

P18 THE TWINS
P24 WICKED CHICKENS
P32 THE LENGTHS
P34 UPCOMING EVENTS
P46 THE BUFFALOS
P48 BROKEN #15
The young lads speak about their success in America
P50 WITTY PINK
Hot new stuff from Witty Pink is on our way!

B *Contents page*

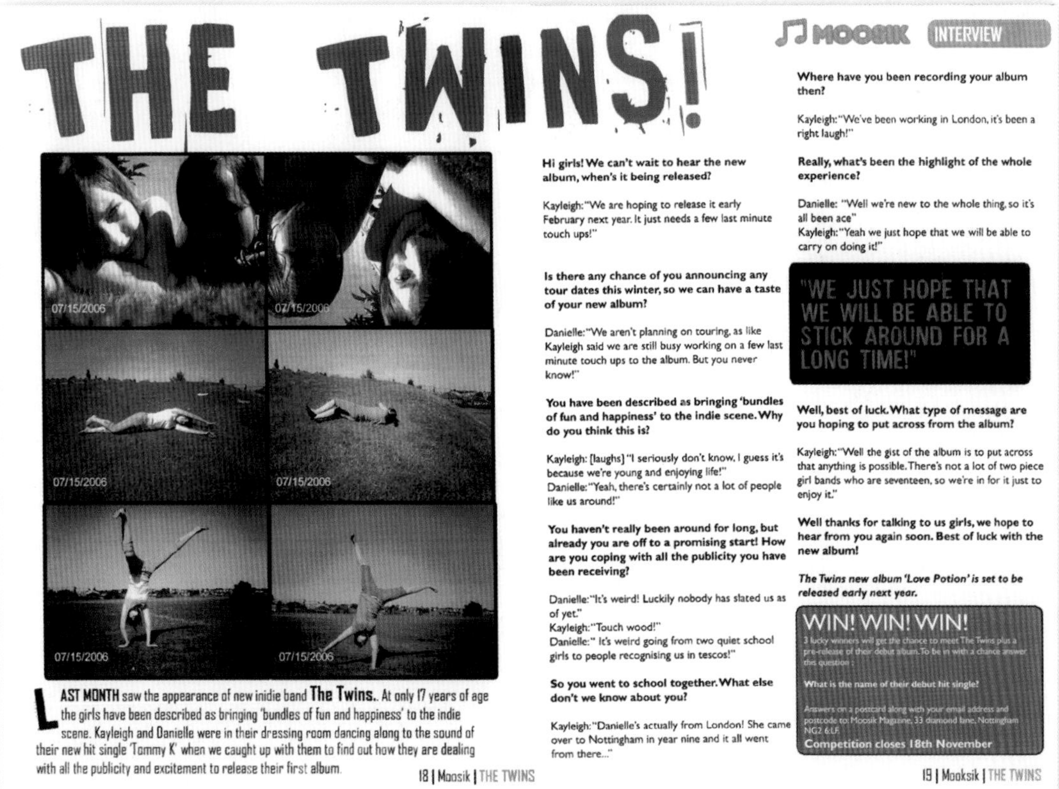
THE TWINS!

MOOSIK INTERVIEW

07/15/2006

LAST MONTH saw the appearance of new inidie band **The Twins.**. At only 17 years of age the girls have been described as bringing 'bundles of fun and happiness' to the indie scene. Kayleigh and Danielle were in their dressing room dancing along to the sound of their new hit single 'Tommy K' when we caught up with them to find out how they are dealing with all the publicity and excitement to release their first album.

Hi girls! We can't wait to hear the new album, when's it being released?

Kayleigh: "We are hoping to release it early February next year. It just needs a few last minute touch ups!"

Is there any chance of you announcing any tour dates this winter, so we can have a taste of your new album?

Danielle: "We aren't planning on touring, as like Kayleigh said we are still busy working on a few last minute touch ups to the album. But you never know!"

You have been described as bringing 'bundles of fun and happiness' to the indie scene. Why do you think this is?

Kayleigh: [laughs] "I seriously don't know. I guess it's because we're young and enjoying life!"
Danielle: "Yeah, there's certainly not a lot of people like us around!"

You haven't really been around for long, but already you are off to a promising start! How are you coping with all the publicity you have been receiving?

Danielle: "It's weird! Luckily nobody has slated us as of yet."
Kayleigh: "Touch wood!"
Danielle: " It's weird going from two quiet school girls to people recognising us in tescos!"

So you went to school together. What else don't we know about you?

Kayleigh: "Danielle's actually from London! She came over to Nottingham in year nine and it all went from there..."

18 | Moosik | THE TWINS

Where have you been recording your album then?

Kayleigh: "We've been working in London, it's been a right laugh!"

Really, what's been the highlight of the whole experience?

Danielle: "Well we're new to the whole thing, so it's all been ace"
Kayleigh: "Yeah we just hope that we will be able to carry on doing it!"

"WE JUST HOPE THAT WE WILL BE ABLE TO STICK AROUND FOR A LONG TIME!"

Well, best of luck. What type of message are you hoping to put across from the album?

Kayleigh: "Well the gist of the album is to put across that anything is possible. There's not a lot of two piece girl bands who are seventeen, so we're in for it just to enjoy it."

Well thanks for talking to us girls, we hope to hear from you again soon. Best of luck with the new album!

The Twins new album 'Love Potion' is set to be released early next year.

WIN! WIN! WIN!
3 lucky winners will get the chance to meet The Twins plus a pre-release of their debut album. To be in with a chance answer this question :
What is the name of their debut hit single?
Answers on a postcard along with your email address and postcode to: Moosik Magazine, 33 diamond lane, Nottingham NG2 6LF.
Competition closes 18th November

19 | Mooksik | THE TWINS

C *Double-page spread*

UNIT ONE Investigating the media

GCSE

The external assessment

Preparing for the written paper

The structure of the external assessment

Topic:	Published every year on the AQA website.
Duration:	1 hour 30 minutes
Tasks:	2 questions (each split into subquestions 1a and 1b; 2a and 2b)
Style of paper:	Pre-released simulation. Unseen questions.
Percentage:	40 per cent of GCSE media studies

Pre-release

The external assessment takes the form of a case study and builds upon the media knowledge and skills that you have developed and demonstrated in Unit 2. The case study will be based on a specific media topic. That topic will change each year and will be published annually on the AQA website. Four weeks before the external assessment, you will be issued with a brief. The brief will set out a simulation which you have an opportunity to research and plan before the external assessment. On the date of the external assessment you will receive the tasks.

How you can prepare for the external assessment

- Although the choice of media topic will change every year, you will need to use and apply the media skills you have learnt during the course. **Develop your media skills.**
- Your school or college should tell you early on in the course the topic of the assessment. You will be expected to have studied this topic in depth, so that you can demonstrate your knowledge in the external assessment. Find out all you can about this topic. **Research the media topic.**
- Do not limit your research to looking at a few websites or textbooks. Try to study the topic by looking at plenty of varied examples. For example, if the topic you are given is science fiction films, you will need to watch a number of these films. If the topic is children's comics, buy some comics and study them. **Look at a wide range of examples from the media topic.**

Objectives

To look at the structure of the external assessment and to learn how to prepare for the written paper.

What you can do when you receive the brief

- Your teacher should read through the brief with you. Look carefully at what it says. The brief will give you some clear guidance about the tasks you will face in the external assessment. **Look for the production task in the brief; plan and prepare your response**.
- The brief may also include some important information about the simulation, such as target audience or ethos of the company. You will need to refer to these points in your answer. **Look carefully for the clues; plan how you will respond**.
- Remember this is a simulation. You will be expected to respond to the brief in role. Responding in role is more than starting your answers with 'Dear Mr XXX'. Instead you will often need to persuade the company in the simulation and sell your ideas. **Plan an in-role response**.
- Continue researching the assessment topic. The brief may help you focus on a particular area of study. **Research the media topic**.

A *Do your research*

How this book can help you research the media topic

While this book does not attempt to cover every area of the media, you may find that the topic area chosen for the external assessment is covered in one of the chapters. Here is a list of topics covered in this book.

Tips for success

Do

- **1 hour 30 minutes** will pass quickly. Give yourself enough time for each question.
- Use the first five minutes to read the questions and make a quick plan of your answers. Remember you should have already prepared some ideas for the production task.
- Make sure you have **read** and **understood** the questions.
- Respond **in role** and to the **brief**.
- Always keep your **target audience** in mind.
- Try to make your production work **interesting and exciting**.
- Use different ways of writing your answers. Mind maps, charts, bullet points and sketches can be very effective in your answers.

Do not

- Spend too much time on one task. Candidates sometimes lose marks because of incomplete responses.
- Spend valuable time colouring in huge sections of production work. If colour is significant, colour in a section of the work as an example. If running out of time, write 'blue masthead' etc.
- Panic. Keep calm and focused on the questions you are being asked.
- Come unprepared. Bring all the equipment you need to the exam venue.

On the next page is a specimen brief on comics. Read it carefully to familiarise yourself with the format of the brief, and take a look at the questions that follow.

kerboodle!

AQA Examination-style questions

Unit 1 specimen brief: children's comics

Pre-released brief

Objectives

To become familiar with the format of a pre-released brief and associated tasks.

Hat Multi Media productions

Applications are invited to join our dynamic digital production team for the launch of our new interactive comic title.

We are planning to produce a weekly online edition aiming to recapture the market share.

We are going to take what was traditionally appealing to youngsters and give it an up-to-date appeal.

We aim to appeal to a new multicultural audience of increasingly sophisticated 7–11 year-olds.

We want to recapture that adventurous spirit and combine it with promoting a healthier lifestyle.

If you think you can contribute to this exciting new venture, phone or email Mick Codis. Details below.

Mick Codis: Creative Manager

mc@hatmultimediaproductions.co.uk

0121323 48446

Completed applications must be submitted by 27 April.

Successful applicants will be expected to offer their ideas for this venture at the interview.

Unit 1 specimen paper: children's comics

The tasks

Congratulations on getting through on the interview stage

In order to make our final choice we need to evaluate your ideas. Complete all the following tasks using the research you have recently undertaken and don't forget to provide plenty of examples in your response.

Task 1 (a) Explain the appeal of print-based comics to their target audience. *(15 marks)*

(b) We need to decide if we are going to proceed with this venture. Explain the advantages and disadvantages of online comics. *(15 marks)*

Task 2 (a) We want to make sure that our new online title will appeal to our target audience. Suggest the key features we need to include to make sure of this appeal. Include any designs you think will make your ideas clear. *(15 marks)*

(b) Design the home page for our new online comic and explain its appeal. Don't forget that it needs to be:

- colourful
- interactive
- attractive to our target audience in terms of both layout and content. *(15 marks)*

Turn the page to find a response to these tasks that would earn you a Grade A.

Unit 1 specimen paper: children's comics

A student response

Objectives

To view a response that would earn a Grade A.

Task 1 (a) Explain the appeal of print-based comics to their target audience. *(15 marks)*

Thanks Mick for your letter. During my research, I have found that people who buy comics are often quite passionate about them. The reasons why people buy them can vary. Using Blumler & Katz's theory of uses and gratifications, I would say people use comics to escape from reality, because the stories are not about real life, for social interaction, as children like to share the experience of reading and swapping comics, and for entertainment with exciting and humorous stories.

An examiner says:

The response is 'in role'. Appropriate media terminology is used.

Also I think certain elements of comics are important to their appeal:

Characters. Characters are a major selling point for comics. Comics have been very successful at creating much-loved comic characters. Some of these characters have been around for many years, and some have been so popular that they have moved into television and film. As they appear in every issue, the audience becomes familiar with them and often develops favourites. Comics like the *Beano* and the *Dandy* have brought us Dennis the Menace, Minnie the Minx and the Bash Street Kids. American comics such as Marvel have bought us Spiderman, Batman and Wonder Woman.

Colour and style. Comics are highly visual; they are colourful and attractive to look at. Comics use few words, but are able to tell funny or exciting stories in a unique style. Bright colours are frequently used. This helps communicate humour and is particularly attractive to young children. More adult comics sometimes use complex and beautiful artwork, such as seen in some Japanese comics. Manga is a very popular and distinctive style used in Japanese comics.

An examiner says:

In both of these parts of the response, intelligent and appropriate illustration is used to support points.

Price. Traditionally comics have been quite cheap to buy. This means that children can use their pocket money to buy them, giving the audience a sense of ownership.

An examiner says:

Good awareness of target audience shows that the demands of the brief are being met.

Covermounts. These days comics frequently have 'free gifts' on the front cover. Cheap, colourful toys are attractive to children, and they are seen as an extra bonus when buying the comic.

Letters pages, competitions and clubs. These give the audience a sense of belonging and loyalty to a comic, as they feel involved.

An examiner says:

A good range of comic conventions are discussed.

Task 1 (b) We need to decide if we are going to proceed with this venture. Explain the advantages and disadvantages of online comics. *(15 marks)*

I think launching a new online comic is a great idea as there are many advantages to this strategy. However there are some disadvantages as well which need some consideration. Here are my ideas.

An examiner says:

Again, response is 'in role' and the task is quickly and confidently addressed.

Advantages

Being 'online' is a great way of bringing interactivity to the comic. The website could include games, clubs, a chat room, and email page. This would be far more immediate and involving compared to letters and competitions by post. The *Beano* has a very interactive website, which includes games, comic strips and competitions.

An examiner says:

Appropriate example given to show how comics and technology have developed.

As some young people have access to the internet on their mobile phones, that would also provide greater access and interactivity.

The characters can be animated and given voices, so some of the comic strips could become cartoons. Or the audience could be able to create their own comic strips, or be given control over a character's actions.

A website has a far bigger potential audience. Most homes these days have access to the internet, and young people often spend a lot of their time online. Hat Multi-media Productions could even aim at a global rather than a national audience.

An online comic would be cheaper to run, as there would be no printing or distribution costs. However, there would obviously be costs involved with setting up and hosting the website.

Our target audience is interested in what is new and modern, and to be purely print based might be seen as rather old fashioned and traditional.

Disadvantages

An online comic would not have the same exposure a print-based comic has. Bright, attractive comic covers are seen on newsagents' shelves and almost sell themselves.

An online comic would need effective advertising so that the audience is aware of its presence and where to access it.

An online comic would not be able to use the appeal of covermounts. Although the website could offer free gifts.

Online comics would lack the mobility of print-based comics. The audience would generally have to be sitting with a computer to access it, whereas a print-based comic can be purchased and read anywhere. Also, an online comic would be consumed in a very different way, and would be unlikely to have a secondary audience, whereas siblings and friends might pick up and read a print-based comic.

Many people like to collect comics. Without a physical print edition, the audience would miss out on this aspect of consuming comics.

An examiner says:

A well-balanced comparison has been made which shows a real understanding of the technological developments which affect audiences and their responses to comics. The material is well organised and clear.

Task 2 (a) We want to make sure that our new online title will appeal to our target audience. Suggest the key features we need to include to make sure of this appeal. Include any designs you think will make your ideas clear. *(15 marks)*

Title

Splash! I think this would be a good title as it suggests fun and action. The title is not gender specific and even suggests some sort of active lifestyle, which would fit in with the healthy living message of the comic. I would use red with yellow edging for the title, as these colours are associated with fun and humour.

Characters

The Fantastic Fruit Five – A mixed group of school children who can change into fruit-based super heroes. They do this by eating their special fruit. Their arch enemies are the Junk Food Gang: a group of unhealthy bullies who always come off worse in their adventures with the Fantastic Fruit Five.

Mick, I think this would meet your brief well because our superheroes could become role models for our audience, and would encourage a healthy diet – 'five a day' could be their catchphrase!

An examiner says:

Comic conventions are evident – catchphrases, arch-enemies, super heroes. References to 'healthy lifestyle' show that the brief has clearly been addressed.

The Splashers. One boy, one girl, different races, who live near the sea. They are expert swimmers and surfers. They are also able to breathe under water, thanks to their uncle's (an inventor) aqua juice. The splashers' adventures often involve saving the marine environment from a nearby baddie oil company.

Mick, again, great characters with a healthy and environmental message.

An examiner says:

Response is again 'in role' (referring to Mick) and these ideas are presented quickly and effectively. Suggestions for narratives show creativity and are appropriate.

Techno boy. A 10-year-old computer wiz who plays tricks on everyone around him. Sometimes his tricks backfire, but always involve hilarious consequences.

Mick, I think this will bring some fun to the comic, and also appeal to children who appreciate modern technology.

The home page needs to be colourful and exciting. The title should be prominent on the home page, and the audience needs clear buttons (links) to take them to the different pages. When the audience finds the home page they need to log on or register to gain access to the rest of the site. This will make it feel more like a club to the audience, and allow us to promote the comic via email to our audience.

An examiner says:

References to audience and trying to create a kind of 'club' show some sophistication and moves this response toward the top of the mark band for Level 6.

Sections

1 Comic strips (characters)

2 Animation

3 Fun stuff (games)

4 Competitions

Competitions – weekly competitions that could involve the audience emailing or texting in their answers. The prizes could include video games, phones and ipods. We could also involve our audience in designing a new character, or deciding on the direction of an ongoing storyline?

Animation – one page of our website could include some aspect of animation where the characters come to life with movement and sound. This could be done quite simply with some *flash* animation.

Fun stuff – one page of our website should include puzzles and games linked to our comic characters. The games could vary in difficulty to appeal to our different ages of audience. Adventure and problem-solving games could be linked to messages of healthy living.

Free give-aways – every week the audience will need to find the magic vegetable (healthy lifestyle) hidden in the website. If they click on it, they will be sent the free gift. These will include tokens to be used at local swimming pools and sports centres.

Task 2 (b) Design the home page for our new online comic and explain its appeal. Don't forget that it needs to be:

- colourful
- interactive
- attractive to our target audience in terms of both layout and content. *(15 marks)*

An examiner says:

Home-page conventions are obvious. The design is appealing and there is evidence of flair. The design is 'colouful, interactive and attractive to (the) target audience' – meeting all of the bullet points of the task.

Throughout all four tasks, the response meets the grade descriptors for the top level (Level 6) and would be worthy of a solid Grade A overall.

Unit 1 specimen brief: fantasy/action films

Pre-released brief

Use this pre-released brief to look for clues that will help you to respond to the four tasks on page 183. Spend some time planning your response. Remember to respond in role.

Apexe Productions

Dear Student,

Here at Apexe Productions we have recently secured funding for a new UK-based film production. Specifically, we are planning the production of a fantasy/action film that features a brand new British superhero character.

We are currently looking for creative young people, to help us lead this exciting project.

We would like you to plan a superhero film that appeals to young people of both genders, that presents a positive role model and is distinct from the current crop of Hollywood superheroes. It would also be important to research the genre of superheroes.

We look forward to hearing your ideas at the end of May.

Good Luck,

Ray Bencuew

Unit 1 specimen brief: fantasy/action films

The tasks

In order to make our final choices we need to evaluate your ideas. Complete the following tasks, using the research you have recently undertaken. Remember to include plenty of examples, and keep your answers sharp and to the point.

Task 1 (a) Show us your understanding of the genre. Explain the different conventions that often feature in Superhero films. *(15 marks)*

(b) In recent years, this genre has proved very successful at the box office. Explain the current popularity of Superhero-based films. *(15 marks)*

Task 2 (a) We want to hear your ideas. In your pitch you may wish to include:

- Title
- Superhero
- A brief outline of the story

You may include sketches to illustrate your ideas.

Explain how your ideas match the brief. *(15 marks)*

(b) We are very interested in the post-release promotion of the film. Produce a mock-up of the DVD front cover for your film. *(15 marks)*

Note

This brief and the associated tasks are based on the format of the AQA specimen paper published in 2008. It is possible that AQA may change this format in the future.

Unit 1 specimen brief: video games

Pre-released brief

Another pre-released brief and tasks to help you tackle the real external assessment with confidence.

QZT GAMES

Dear Student,

Thank you for your application. As you know we are currently looking to launch a new range of games to be released on all the major formats.

We are interested in producing games that are exciting, challenging but also include an element of education. Games should also include some form of story and an element of problem solving.

While we are mainly targeting a teenage audience, we are keen for our games to appeal to both genders.

Before we see your ideas, you'll need to spend some time finding out about the gaming industry.

Yours sincerely,

Cara Flort

Unit 1 specimen brief: video games

The tasks

Task 1 (a) From your knowledge of the gaming industry, explain what makes a successful game. You should include plenty of examples to illustrate your answer. *(15 marks)*

(b) In recent years there has been much controversy surrounding the gaming industry. Explain why some games have been criticised in the media. *(15 marks)*

Task 2 (a) Give an outline of your game.

Remember to explain how it will appeal to the target audience and how it meets the needs of the brief. You may include sketches to illustrate your ideas. *(15 marks)*

(b) We want the game to have a dynamic and exciting beginning.

Storyboard the opening sequence of the game. This should last for 30 seconds. *(15 marks)*

Note

This brief and the associated tasks are based on the format of the AQA specimen paper published in 2008. It is possible that AQA may change this format in the future.

Glossary

A

ABCe Unique Users figure: tells you how many different people visit a magazine's website in a month.

Anti-hero: usually the main character who the audience cheer on but who has a number of negative characteristics.

Appeal: something attractive or interesting that will grab and hold your audience's attention, and make them come back to your website again.

Audience: one of the key concepts; the people who consume a media text.

B

Blog: a website where entries are made in journal style. Blogs can be found on all different topics. Sometimes they are called 'web logs'.

Broadsheet: printed in a large format (74 cm × 59 cm approx.); broadsheets are more serious and detailed in their news coverage.

C

Champion theme: sets the tone for individual advertisements and other forms of marketing communications that will be used in an advertising campaign.

Codes and conventions: the typical features that we would expect from a particular text, the 'rules'.

Connotation: the message that a media text might give or suggest.

Contingency plan: a plan that can be put in place for an event or circumstance that is possible but might not happen.

Copy: a printed article in a newspaper.

Core audience: the main, expected audience for a media text.

Covert advertising: when a product or brand is clearly visible or often referred to in a television programme or film; sometimes called product placement.

Cross-media campaign: when the same text appears on a range of different platforms. For instance, the release of a new film will result in a media-wide campaign with material generated across different forms, such as television, radio, magazines, newspapers and the internet.

Cult: a group of devoted followers that sets itself apart from a main group.

Cut: an immediate change from one image to another.

D

Demographics: measurement of the population in terms of age, sex, religion, income, ethnicity, etc.

Denotation: what we can see in a media text.

Diegetic sound: a sound that we might expect to hear in a particular scene.

Digital space: any multimedia-enabled electronic channel that an advertiser's message can be seen or heard from.

Drop cap: the first letter of a paragraph that is enlarged to 'drop' down two or more lines.

E

Elements: the individual parts that together make up a web page.

Entry point: small bits of information or visual interest designed to catch the eye and give a quick fix of content that leaves the reader wanting more.

Establishing shot: to show the audience a change of location, a still shot of the exterior of a location will be shown.

Extract: in this case, a part of a television programme or film that lasts for no more than five minutes.

Eyetrack III: a company that has developed a technique to determine where a person is looking.

F

Flat plan: a page plan that shows the position of all the articles.

Font: the style of lettering used.

Fourth wall: when filmed in a TV studio, a sitcom will usually only show three walls. For instance, in *Friends*, when the Central Park set is used, the camera (and therefore the audience) will always occupy the fourth wall.

Frames: the boxes or shapes in which the text and drawings of the comic appear.

G

Genre: from the French meaning 'type'. When we talk about a genre of film, we might refer to science fiction, romantic comedy or several other 'types' of film.

Grossing: refers to money made at the box office.

H

High-key: very bright lighting which creates a glossy look that can give a glamorous feel but may seem artificial.

Home page: the first page of a website that the user will come across. This page usually contains links to other pages on the website.

House style: the identity of a media product which makes it easily recognisable to its audience.

I

Index: the National Readership Survey interviews approximately 30 000 people a year about their reading habits. From this an index is compiled. Figures over 100 show that readers are 'more likely' than non-readers to fit a certain profile.

Institutions: one of the key concepts; the organisations that are responsible for producing media products.

Integrated marketing communication: an attempt to ensure that information about a product or service is effectively distributed to the intended audience.

Intertextuality: where one media text makes reference to another.

Internet Service Provider (ISP): a company that collects a monthly or annual fee in exchange for providing the subscriber with internet access.

K

Key concepts: in GCSE Media Studies these are media language, audience, representation and institutions.

L

Layout: the way that the different elements of a page are set out.

Linear narrative: a storyline that progresses in chronological order from beginning to end.

Low-key: refers to any scene with a high lighting ratio. It is often used in horror films to create a shadowy atmosphere.

Lures: attempts to attract the audience or reader by offering something.

M

Masthead: the title of a newspaper, magazine or website positioned at the top of the front cover or home page.

Media form: the distinguishing characteristics of types of media products.

Media language: one of the key concepts; the technical terms associated with each media form.

Media platform: the technology through which we receive media products.

Mode of address: the 'feel' a media text gives to an audience.

Mood boards: used to give a sense of the style or the 'mood' of the work. They are often presented as a collection of colours, text and images that, when combined, communicate a design idea.

MTV: Music TeleVision; MTV was launched in the USA, in 1981.

N

Narrative: the story – a sequence of events.

News values: the criteria newspaper editors use for selecting news stories.

Non-diegetic sound: a sound that does not normally belong in a particular scene.

P

Panning: the camera is fixed at a particular point, perhaps using a tripod, but then moves from left to right (or right to left) as your eyes might as you survey a landscape.

Paparazzi: photographers who specialise in taking candid pictures of celebrities.

Parody: an imitation.

Photojournalist: a journalist who uses photographs to tell a story.

Pitch: where a writer explains and tries to sell his or her idea for a media product to a producer.

POV (point of view): for the first drawing in the storyboard, Martin Asbury has referred to Rachel's POV. In other words, the camera is showing what the character Rachel can see.

Promotional activities: activities that attempt to raise awareness of a product or service.

Pull quotes: quotations from an article that are placed in a larger font, on the same page, to entice the reader into the story.

R

Representation: one of the key concepts; how people, events and ideas are presented to audiences.

Rupture of verisimilitude: verisimilitude means the attempt by film-makers to show reality or normality. This is ruptured (or broken) when something clearly unrealistic happens. Talking directly to the viewers would be an example of this.

S

Script: the written text of a play, film or broadcast.

Secondary audience: not the main, expected audience for a media text but another group who might be part of the audience. For instance, teenage girls' magazines sometimes interest the brothers or boyfriends of the main target audience. They are a secondary audience.

Sell lines: on a magazine front cover, the writing that appears around the main image and which tells readers what is inside the magazine.

Serif: a slight projection finishing off the stroke of a letter. Letters presented in a serif font are curly and appear traditional or old fashioned.

Sitcom: means 'situation comedy'; a television genre.

Slug: a short heading indicating the subject of the copy.

Stereotyping: the portrayal of people or places through a few obvious characteristics.

Storyboarding: often used as a planning tool by professional film makers. It involves drawing a sequence of illustrations that represents the shots planned for a film or television production.

Sub-genre: an identifiable sub-class from a larger film genre. For example, a martial arts film is a type of action film.

Sub-plot: a less important story than the main plot.

Synergy: the process by which a media institution uses different products to sell another (e.g. film, video game, soundtrack).

T

Tabloid: a size of newspaper (43 cm × 28 cm approx.); tabloids traditionally are more sensationalist and less serious in their news coverage.

Tag line: a memorable slogan or phrase that will sum up the tone of a brand or product.

Tracking: the camera moves with a subject, so that the subject stays in the centre of a shot. In feature films this is likely to be achieved by constructing a track on which the camera will move (a dolly track).

Turkey: a film that performs very badly at the box office.

U

Uses and gratifications: a theory suggested by Blumler and Katz to explain the reasons why audiences consume media texts.

USP (unique selling point): an aspect of a product that makes it distinct from similar products.

V

Viral marketing: marketing that encourages people to pass on marketing messages through emails and texts.

Index